Speak the Word: Nurturing Hearts and Transforming Lives

Andrew J. Lamont-Turner

Published by Andrew J. Lamont-Turner, 2024.

While every precaution has been taken in the preparation of this book, the publisher assumes no responsibility for errors or omissions, or for damages resulting from the use of the information contained herein.

SPEAK THE WORD: NURTURING HEARTS AND TRANSFORMING LIVES

First edition. April 3, 2024.

Copyright © 2024 Andrew J. Lamont-Turner.

ISBN: 979-8224539413

Written by Andrew J. Lamont-Turner.

Table of Contents

Introduction

—————

Welcome to "Speak the Word: Nurturing Hearts and Transforming Lives." In this book, we embark on a journey that explores the transformative power of preaching and equips preachers with practical tools and insights to deliver impactful sermons.

Preaching is an ancient and sacred art rooted in the rich tradition of proclaiming God's Word to His people. It is a calling that carries great responsibility—the responsibility to communicate God's truth, engage hearts, challenge minds, and inspire lives. Whether you are a seasoned preacher or just beginning your ministry journey, this book aims to empower you with the knowledge, skills, and inspiration to become a more effective herald of the Word.

This comprehensive guide delves into the fundamental aspects of preaching, examining the biblical basis, significance, and purpose of this sacred task. We explore the vital connection between the preacher's personal character, spiritual life, and the impact of their message. We delve into the sermon preparation process, from engaging in rigorous exegesis and hermeneutics to understanding the historical and literary context of the text. We discuss the importance of planning a preaching series, choosing relevant and impactful texts, and structuring sermons to captivate and engage the congregation.

Crafting the sermon is an art in itself, and we provide practical tips on developing themes, creating clear and effective outlines, and incorporating illustrations and applications that resonate with the listeners' lives. The book also explores the nuances of sermon delivery, from effective communication techniques to engaging body language and overcoming nerves and distractions. We delve into the essential skill of evaluating sermons through personal reflection and feedback from others, enabling preachers to continually grow and improve in their ministry.

Recognising the diversity of contexts in which preaching occurs, we explore the challenges and opportunities of preaching to different age groups, non-Christian audiences, and various cultural settings. We also examine the integral role of preaching in the church's life as an act of worship, discipleship, and evangelism, fostering a deep appreciation for the significance of this sacred task.

As we navigate the pages of this book, we also address the contemporary challenges to biblical authority and the cultural changes that impact preaching today. We explore the opportunities for Gospel impact in a rapidly changing world, encouraging preachers to boldly proclaim the unchanging truth in relevant and impactful ways.

Ultimately, "Speak the Word: Nurturing Hearts and Transforming Lives" seeks to inspire preachers with a vision for the future of preaching, urging them to embrace their calling with passion, authenticity, and unwavering dedication. May this book serve as a valuable resource and source of encouragement, empowering preachers to unleash the transformative power of God's Word, nurture souls, and impact lives for the glory of His Kingdom.

1. Introduction to Preaching

In a world where communication takes various forms and platforms, preaching is a timeless and profound method of conveying truth, inspiring hearts, and transforming lives. At its core, preaching is an art form that combines the power of language, the wisdom of Scripture, and the preacher's passion to engage with an audience in a way that illuminates and imparts profound spiritual truths.

Definition of Preaching: To embark on a journey into preaching, it is crucial to establish a clear understanding of what preaching entails. Preaching can be defined as communicating God's message to a gathered assembly, whether it be a congregation within a religious setting, a community seeking spiritual guidance, or an audience hungry for moral and ethical insight. It involves the proclamation of divine truth, interpreting sacred texts, and applying biblical principles to listeners' lives.

Importance of Preaching: Why is preaching so significant? Preaching has shaped societies, fostered spiritual growth, and ignited social change. It can challenge, comfort, and convict individuals, transcending cultural, linguistic, and generational barriers. Preaching serves as a conduit for divine revelation, offering guidance, hope, and a call to transformation. It can awaken dormant faith, awaken the conscience, and inspire action.

Biblical Basis for Preaching: The foundation of preaching lies deeply rooted in the Scriptures, serving as a divine mandate and a rich source of inspiration. From the ancient prophets passionately proclaiming God's message to the apostles fearlessly preaching the gospel of Jesus Christ, the Bible exemplifies the transformative power of spoken truth.

Preaching originates in the teachings of Jesus Himself, who commissioned His disciples to "go into all the world and preach the gospel to all creation" (Mark 16:15). Throughout the New Testament, preaching and teaching are emphasised to edify believers, equip them for service, and share the good news with the world.

As we explore preaching, we will explore various aspects contributing to its effectiveness and impact. From the foundational elements of the preacher's personal character and spiritual life to the practical skills of sermon preparation, delivery, and evaluation, this book aims to equip aspiring and seasoned preachers with the tools necessary to engage, inspire, and transform lives through the spoken word.

Join us as we embark on a journey that explores the depths of preaching, its significance in the life of the church and society, and its enduring relevance in a rapidly changing world. Together, let us rediscover the art and power of preaching and embrace its calling to illuminate hearts, shape minds, and draw individuals closer to the truth that sets them free.

Definition of Preaching

To understand the essence of preaching, it is essential to clearly define this profound act of communication. Preaching can be defined as the proclamation and communication of God's message to a gathered assembly to instruct, inspire, challenge, and encourage listeners in their faith journey.

The Bible provides us with insights into the nature and purpose of preaching. Throughout the Old and New Testaments, we encounter numerous examples of individuals who were called to preach and teach about the significance of this ministry.

In the Old Testament, the Hebrew word most commonly associated with preaching is "qara," which means to proclaim, call out, or announce. The prophets, in particular, were often called to fulfil the role of preachers, delivering messages directly from God to His people. Their preaching involved both proclaiming God's judgment and offering hope for restoration. They acted as God's messengers, faithfully communicating His will and speaking truth to the people.

For instance, in the book of Jeremiah, the prophet is explicitly called to preach: "Then the Lord reached out his hand and touched my mouth and said to me, 'I have put my words in your mouth. See, today I appoint you over nations and kingdoms to uproot and tear down, to destroy and overthrow, to build and to plant'" (Jeremiah 1:9-10). Jeremiah's preaching ministry involved delivering difficult messages of judgment and warning to the people of Israel, calling them to repentance and faithfulness to God.

In the New Testament, the Greek word commonly used for preaching is "kērussō," meaning proclaiming, heralding, or announcing. Jesus

Himself embodied the essence of preaching as He travelled throughout Galilee, teaching in synagogues and proclaiming the good news of the Kingdom (Matthew 4:23, Mark 1:14-15).

Jesus commissioned His disciples to continue the work of preaching: "Go into all the world and preach the gospel to all creation" (Mark 16:15). This command reflects the divine mandate to proclaim the message of salvation, calling all people to repentance, faith in Christ, and reconciliation with God and one another.

The apostle Paul, who significantly spread the gospel throughout the Mediterranean, embraced the preaching calling wholeheartedly. In his letters, he emphasises the importance of preaching to communicate God's redemptive plan. He writes to the Corinthians, stating, "For Christ did not send me to baptise but to preach the gospel—not with wisdom and eloquence, lest the cross of Christ is emptied of its power" (1 Corinthians 1:17). Paul understood that the power of preaching lies not in human eloquence or persuasion but in the proclamation of the cross, which brings salvation and transforms lives.

The apostle Paul encourages his protege Timothy, who was engaged in the work of preaching, to devote himself to this task: "Preach the word; be prepared in season and out of season; correct, rebuke and encourage—with great patience and careful instruction" (2 Timothy 4:2). Paul recognises preaching as a responsibility that requires preparation, fidelity to God's Word, and a commitment to transforming hearers' lives.

In summary, the biblical understanding of preaching encompasses the proclamation of God's message, calling people to repentance, faith, and a transformed life. Preaching is not a mere performance or intellectual exercise but a divine assignment entrusted to individuals called by God to communicate His truth. Preachers are tasked with faithfully expounding the Scriptures, challenging and encouraging listeners to align their lives with the teachings of Jesus Christ.

As we explore the multifaceted aspects of preaching, it is crucial to recognise that preaching should always be grounded in the authority and truth of God's Word. It is not the words of human wisdom but the power of God that brings about conviction, repentance, and spiritual growth (1 Corinthians 2:4-5). Preaching, when carried out with humility, dependence on the Holy Spirit, and a sincere desire to see lives transformed, can catalyse spiritual renewal, community building, and the advancement of God's Kingdom.

Importance of Preaching

—————

Preaching holds immense importance in the spiritual journey of individuals and the church's life. It serves as a vital communication between God and His people, providing guidance, encouragement, correction, and inspiration. Let's delve deeper into the significance of preaching and explore its biblical foundation.

Throughout the Bible, we witness numerous examples of preaching as a powerful tool for transformation. The Old Testament prophets, such as Isaiah, Jeremiah, and Ezekiel, faithfully proclaimed God's message to the people of Israel, calling them to repentance, revealing God's promises, and warning of impending judgment. Their words carried divine authority and impacted the lives of both individuals and nations.

In the New Testament, Jesus Himself is the ultimate model of a preacher. His ministry was characterised by powerful preaching, as He declared the arrival of the Kingdom of God, taught profound truths through parables, and called people to repentance and faith. Jesus' Sermon on the Mount (Matthew 5-7) remains a pinnacle of His preaching, encompassing principles that continue to guide and challenge believers today.

The early church in the Book of Acts provides a compelling example of the importance of preaching. The apostles, filled with the Holy Spirit, boldly proclaimed the gospel message, converting thousands of souls. On the day of Pentecost, the apostle Peter delivered a powerful sermon (Acts 2:14-41), resulting in three thousand people embracing faith in Christ. The book of Acts records numerous instances of preaching as a catalyst for spiritual awakening, growth, and the expansion of the early Christian movement.

The epistles of the New Testament also emphasise the significance of preaching in the church's life. The apostle Paul, in his letters to Timothy and Titus, instructs them regarding the importance of sound doctrine, teaching, and preaching (1 Timothy 4:13, 2 Timothy 2:15, Titus 2:1). He underscores the transformative power of the gospel message, proclaiming it as the "power of God that brings salvation" (Romans 1:16).

The importance of preaching is not limited to the early church. It continues to hold relevance in the present age. Preaching serves as a means of edification, equipping believers for service and nurturing spiritual growth (Ephesians 4:11-16). It provides a platform for the proclamation of the gospel to believers and non-believers, challenging and encouraging individuals to live in alignment with God's Word.

In the church context, preaching can unite believers, foster a shared understanding of biblical truths, and inspire a collective response to God's calling. It is a means through which the Word of God is made accessible, applicable, and relevant to the lives of believers, providing guidance and direction for daily living.

It is important to note that preaching is not confined to a specific format or setting. While it often occurs within a church's walls during a worship service, preaching can also occur in various contexts, such as evangelistic crusades, conferences, small group gatherings, and even through digital platforms. The essence of preaching lies in the faithful proclamation of God's truth, irrespective of the medium used.

The importance of preaching is deeply rooted in the biblical narrative and the teachings of Jesus and the early church. It is a means through which God's message is communicated, hearts are transformed, and lives are impacted. Preaching catalyses spiritual growth, the gospel's spread, and the believers' edification. As preachers faithfully handle God's Word, they have the privilege and responsibility to convey divine truth, guiding individuals toward a deeper understanding of God's plan and purpose for their lives. Through preaching, believers are challenged to live out their faith, find hope in times of despair, and draw closer to God.

The importance of preaching extends beyond individual transformation. It plays a vital role in the church's life, fostering unity, providing spiritual nourishment, and equipping believers for service. As the Word of God is faithfully proclaimed, the church is built up, guided, and empowered to fulfil its mission of making disciples and advancing the Kingdom of God.

Preaching is a beacon of truth in a world marked by shifting values, moral relativism, and spiritual hunger. It offers a counter-narrative to the voices of the culture, pointing people to the unchanging Word of God. Through preaching, individuals are confronted with the reality of sin, offered the gift of salvation through Jesus Christ, and invited to experience the transformative power of the Holy Spirit.

As preachers faithfully engage in preaching, they participate in God's redemptive work, serving as vessels through which divine truth is communicated. They have the privilege of speaking on behalf of God, guiding people into a deeper understanding of His character, His will, and His purposes. Preaching is a reminder of God's Word's living and active nature, capable of penetrating hearts, convicting consciences, and inspiring lives.

The importance of preaching cannot be overstated. It is a sacred calling that requires a deep reverence for God, a thorough understanding of His Word, and a genuine love for His people. Preachers are entrusted with the responsibility of faithfully proclaiming the message of God, allowing His truth to shine through their words and actions.

As we delve into the depths of preaching, exploring its various aspects and practicalities, let us approach this task with humility, prayer, and a deep dependence on the Holy Spirit. May this exploration equip and inspire preachers to engage in the noble art of preaching, knowing that through their faithful proclamation, lives will be transformed, communities will be impacted, and God's Kingdom will be advanced.

Biblical Basis for Preaching

The biblical basis for preaching is rooted in the Scriptures, which reveal the divine mandate and exemplify the transformative power of spoken truth. Throughout the Old and New Testaments, we find evidence of the significance and authority of preaching to communicate God's message to His people.

In the Old Testament, we see the role of prophets as preachers of God's word. God called them to deliver His messages, warnings, and promises to the people of Israel. The prophet Jeremiah, for example, describes his experience of being called by God to preach: "The word of the Lord came to me, saying, 'Before I formed you in the womb, I knew you, before you were born, I set you apart; I appointed you as a prophet to the nations'" (Jeremiah 1:4-5). This passage illustrates the divine commissioning of Jeremiah as a preacher, highlighting the preexistence of God's plan and purpose for his life.

The prophets' preaching was not limited to foretelling future events; it also involved calling people to repentance, obedience, and faithfulness to God's covenant. The book of Isaiah presents a powerful example of prophetic preaching, as Isaiah proclaims God's judgment and promises of restoration to a rebellious nation. Through his preaching, Isaiah implores the people to turn away from their sinful ways and embrace God's righteousness (Isaiah 1:16-20).

In the New Testament, Jesus Himself is the ultimate model of a preacher. His ministry was marked by powerful preaching, as He declared the arrival of the Kingdom of God, taught profound truths through parables, and called people to repentance and faith. Jesus' inaugural sermon in Nazareth, as recorded in Luke 4:16-21, showcases

His proclamation of the fulfilment of Old Testament prophecies and His identification as the Anointed One. Jesus' preaching was persuasive and transformative, as it challenged societal norms, offered hope to the marginalised, and called for a radical reorientation of values.

The commission to preach continued with the apostles whom Jesus chose and equipped to carry on His ministry. The book of Acts portrays their boldness in preaching the gospel to the Jewish people and the Gentiles. In Acts 2, we witness the apostle Peter's sermon on the day of Pentecost, where he proclaims the fulfilment of Joel's prophecy and points to Jesus as the Messiah. His preaching added three thousand souls to the early church (Acts 2:41).

The apostle Paul, known as the "apostle to the Gentiles," emphasises the centrality of preaching in his ministry. He acknowledges the power of preaching in bringing about faith and salvation: "For it is by grace you have been saved, through faith—and this is not from yourselves, it is the gift of God—not by works so that no one can boast" (Ephesians 2:8-9). Paul's preaching was characterised by the proclamation of Christ crucified and risen, the demonstration of God's love and grace, and the call to a life transformed by the power of the Holy Spirit.

The New Testament epistles also highlight the importance of sound teaching and preaching within the early church context. The apostle Paul exhorts his protégé Timothy to be diligent in his preaching and teaching ministry, emphasising the authority and sufficiency of Scripture: "All Scripture is God-breathed and is useful for teaching, rebuking, correcting, and training in righteousness, so that the servant of God may be thoroughly equipped for every good work" (2 Timothy 3:16-17). This passage underscores the foundational role of Scripture in preaching, affirming its divine inspiration and its capacity to instruct, correct, and equip believers for a life of obedience and service.

The biblical basis for preaching extends beyond the examples and teachings of specific individuals. It rests upon the inherent authority and power of God's Word itself. The writer of Hebrews declares, "For the word of God is alive and active. Sharper than any double-edged sword, it penetrates even to dividing soul and spirit, joints and marrow; it judges the thoughts and attitudes of the heart" (Hebrews 4:12). This verse emphasises the dynamic nature of Scripture, which is capable of penetrating hearts, exposing hidden motives, and bringing about transformation in the lives of hearers.

Preaching is not merely an exercise in human eloquence or persuasive rhetoric. It is a means by which the living Word of God is proclaimed and applied to the lives of individuals and communities. It invites people to encounter the truth and power of God's Word, leading to repentance, faith, and a deeper relationship with Him.

As preachers engage in preaching, they are called to handle God's Word with reverence, accuracy, and faithfulness. The apostle Paul charges Timothy, saying, "Do your best to present yourself to God as one approved, a worker who does not need to be ashamed and who correctly handles the word of truth" (2 Timothy 2:15). This admonition highlights the responsibility of preachers to diligently study and rightly interpret Scripture, ensuring that their preaching aligns with its intended meaning and purpose.

Ultimately, the biblical basis for preaching affirms its central role in God's redemptive plan. It is a means by which God speaks to His people, convicts hearts, brings about repentance, imparts knowledge and understanding, and equips believers for service. Through the faithful proclamation of God's Word, preachers participate in the ongoing work of God's Kingdom, bringing light into darkness, hope into despair, and salvation to the lost.

As we delve into the depths of preaching, let us approach this sacred task with humility, prayer, and a deep dependence on the Holy Spirit. May our preaching be rooted in the authority of God's Word, marked by clarity, integrity, and an unwavering commitment to faithfully proclaiming the message of salvation. May it lead to the transformation of lives, the edification of the church, and the advancement of God's Kingdom on earth.

2. Preparing to Preach

Effective preaching requires careful and intentional preparation. Preparing to preach involves cultivating personal character, seeking spiritual guidance, studying and interpreting the Scriptures, and understanding the historical and literary context of the text. These elements contribute to the preacher's ability to communicate God's message effectively with clarity, relevance, and transformative power.

In this section, we will explore the various aspects of preparing to preach, recognising that the preacher's role is not limited to delivering a sermon but extends to a commitment to a life of integrity, spiritual growth, and ongoing learning. Preparing to preach is an ongoing journey of deepening one's relationship with God, growing in knowledge and understanding of His Word, and honing the skills necessary for effective communication.

First and foremost, the preacher's personal character and spiritual life play a crucial role in preparing to preach. The preacher is called to be a vessel through which God's message flows. Cultivating a life of authenticity, humility, and dependence on God is essential. The preacher's personal relationship with God, characterised by prayer, worship, and the study of Scripture, provides the foundation for the preaching ministry. Jesus emphasises the importance of abiding in Him, saying, "I am the vine; you are the branches. If you remain in me and I in you, you will bear much fruit; apart from me, you can do nothing" (John 15:5). The preacher's connection with God directly impacts their ability to effectively communicate His message.

The preacher's dependence on the Holy Spirit is paramount. The Holy Spirit guides, empowers, and illuminates the preacher's understanding of Scripture, enabling them to discern and effectively convey its truths. Jesus assures His disciples, "But the Advocate, the Holy Spirit, whom the Father will send in my name, will teach you all things and remind you of everything I have said to you" (John 14:26). The preacher relies on the Holy Spirit's guidance and inspiration throughout the entire process of sermon preparation.

A crucial aspect of preparing to preach involves diligently studying and interpreting the Scriptures. The preacher is called to rightly handle the Word of God (2 Timothy 2:15) and to accurately convey its intended meaning and message. This necessitates a commitment to studying the Scriptures in depth, employing tools of exegesis and hermeneutics to understand the text's historical, cultural, and literary context. The apostle Paul encourages Timothy, saying, "Do your best to present yourself to God as one approved, a worker who does not need to be ashamed and who correctly handles the word of truth" (2 Timothy 2:15). The preacher's dedication to diligent study ensures the faithful representation and application of God's Word.

Understanding the historical and literary context of the text is vital for interpreting and communicating its message effectively. Each passage of Scripture is embedded within a specific historical setting, written by authors with distinct styles, themes, and purposes. The preacher gains insights into the original audience's cultural background, challenges, and expectations by delving into the historical context. Likewise, understanding the literary context helps the preacher discern the text's genre, structure, and flow. These contextual considerations allow the preacher to illuminate the original meaning and bridge the gap between the ancient biblical world and the contemporary audience.

Preparing to preach requires a holistic approach that encompasses personal character development, spiritual growth, diligent study, and contextual understanding. The preacher's preparation involves cultivating a vibrant relationship with God, relying on the guidance of the Holy Spirit, studying the Scriptures with diligence, and discerning the historical and literary context of the text. As preachers commit themselves to this preparation process, they position themselves to effectively communicate God's message with clarity, relevance, and transformative power. Preparing to preach is not a task to be taken lightly but a sacred responsibility that requires a deep commitment to personal growth and an unwavering dedication to faithfully proclaiming the Word of God.

In the upcoming sections, we will delve into each aspect of preparing to preach in greater detail. We will explore the importance of personal character and spiritual life, offering practical insights and guidance on cultivating a vibrant and authentic relationship with God. We will discuss the role of prayer and dependence on the Holy Spirit in seeking divine guidance and empowerment for the preaching ministry. We will delve into the methodologies of exegesis and hermeneutics, equipping preachers with tools to rightly interpret and understand the Scriptures. Finally, we will explore the significance of understanding the historical and literary context of the text, providing strategies for bridging the gap between the ancient biblical world and the modern audience.

As we embark on this journey of preparing to preach, let us approach it with humility, reverence, and a genuine desire to faithfully communicate God's truth. May our preparation be marked by a deep love for God and His Word, a commitment to personal growth, and an unwavering dedication to serving as faithful stewards of the preaching ministry. Through diligent preparation, we can strive to present ourselves as approved workers, accurately handling the Word of truth and effectively impacting the lives of those who hear. May the power of God's Word be proclaimed with conviction, clarity, and transformational impact as we prepare to preach the unchanging truth in a changing world.

Personal Character and Spiritual Life of the Preacher

The preacher's personal character and spiritual life are foundational to effective preaching. The preacher's character serves as a reflection of their relationship with God. It influences the credibility, authenticity, and impact of their message. Developing a Christlike character and nurturing a vibrant spiritual life is essential for preachers to effectively represent God and His Word to the congregation.

Jesus emphasised the importance of inner transformation and character development when He said, "A good man brings good things out of the good stored up in his heart, and an evil man brings evil things out of the evil stored up in his heart. For the mouth speaks what the heart is full of" (Luke 6:45). This verse underscores the significance of cultivating a heart aligned with God's truth and values. The preacher's words and actions should flow from a heart transformed by the love and grace of God.

The preacher's character should reflect the fruits of the Holy Spirit, as described by the apostle Paul in Galatians 5:22-23: "But the fruit of the Spirit is love, joy, peace, forbearance, kindness, goodness, faithfulness, gentleness, and self-control." These qualities should be evident in the preacher's interactions with others within and outside the church community. Preachers are called to model Christlikeness in their relationships, displaying humility, integrity, and a genuine concern for the well-being of others.

The preacher's spiritual life is intimately connected to their ability to effectively communicate God's message. Spending time praying, studying the Scriptures, and cultivating a deep relationship with God are vital aspects of nurturing a vibrant spiritual life. Jesus Himself set an example of seeking solitude and communion with the Father through prayer. In Mark 1:35, it is written, "Very early in the morning, while it was still dark, Jesus got up, left the house, and went off to a solitary place, where he prayed." This demonstrates the significance of regular and intentional prayer in the life of a preacher.

Studying and reflecting on the Scriptures is another crucial aspect of the preacher's spiritual life. The psalmist declares, "I have hidden your word in my heart that I might not sin against you" (Psalm 119:11). The preacher should immerse themselves in the Word of God, allowing it to shape their thoughts, attitudes, and actions. Through a deep understanding of Scripture, the preacher gains insight into God's character, His redemptive plan, and the timeless truths to be proclaimed from the pulpit.

The preacher's spiritual life should be characterised by ongoing growth and transformation. The apostle Peter exhorts believers to "grow in the grace and knowledge of our Lord and Savior Jesus Christ" (2 Peter 3:18). Preachers should be committed to a lifelong journey of personal growth, continuously seeking a deeper understanding of God's Word, maturing in their faith, and allowing the Holy Spirit to shape their character.

The preacher's personal character and spiritual life influence their relationship with God and the congregation's perception of the message they proclaim. A preacher who lives a life of integrity, authenticity, and humility enhances their credibility and fosters a greater impact on the lives of those who listen. Conversely, a preacher whose character contradicts their message may hinder the reception and effectiveness of their preaching.

The preacher's personal character and spiritual life are integral to effective preaching. As preachers strive to cultivate Christlike character and nurture a vibrant spiritual life, they reflect God's love, grace, and truth to the congregation. By modelling humility, integrity, and a genuine love for God and others, preachers create an environment where the message of the Gospel can be received with greater openness and receptivity.

Preachers need to recognise that their character and spiritual life are not developed in isolation but within the context of community and accountability. The apostle Paul encourages believers to spur one another toward love and good deeds, emphasising the importance of gathering together for mutual edification and growth (Hebrews 10:24-25). Preachers should actively seek support and encouragement from fellow believers, participating in mentorship, discipleship, and accountability relationships that help nurture their character and spiritual well-being.

As preachers prioritise the development of their personal character and spiritual life, they position themselves to effectively serve God and His people. Their transformed lives become a living testimony of God's work, allowing the congregation to see the power of the Gospel at work in the preacher's own journey. Through their authenticity, humility, and commitment to personal growth, preachers create an atmosphere where the congregation is encouraged to pursue their relationship with God and embrace the transformative power of His Word.

In the next sections, we will delve deeper into the practices and disciplines contributing to the preacher's character and spiritual life. We will explore the significance of prayer and dependence on the Holy Spirit in seeking divine guidance and empowerment. We will also discuss the importance of ongoing study and reflection on the Scriptures and the role of community and accountability in fostering personal growth. By engaging in these disciplines, preachers can continually develop their character, deepen their spiritual life, and become more effective instruments in proclaiming the life-changing message of God's Word.

Prayer and Dependence on the Holy Spirit

Prayer and dependence on the Holy Spirit are essential to preparing to preach. They provide the foundation for effective communication of God's Word, enabling the preacher to align their thoughts, words, and actions with God's purposes. Through prayer, the preacher seeks divine guidance, empowerment, and anointing, recognising their need for the Holy Spirit to work in and through them.

Jesus Himself modelled the importance of prayer and dependence on the Holy Spirit in His ministry. Before selecting His disciples, He prayed all night (Luke 6:12-13). Throughout His earthly ministry, Jesus frequently withdrew to solitary places to pray and seek communion with the Father (Luke 5:16). Prayer was an integral part of Jesus' life and ministry, demonstrating His reliance on the Father for wisdom, strength, and direction.

Likewise, preachers are called to emulate Jesus' example by prioritising prayer in their lives. Through prayer, preachers can align their hearts with God's will, discern His purposes, and seek guidance in preparing and delivering sermons. Prayer provides an opportunity to surrender personal agendas, biases, and insecurities, allowing the Holy Spirit to work through the preacher with clarity, conviction, and power.

The apostle Paul emphasises the significance of prayer in the life of a preacher. In his letter to the Ephesian believers, he writes, "And pray in the Spirit on all occasions with all kinds of prayers and requests. With this in mind, be alert and always pray for all the Lord's people. Pray also for me, that words may be given whenever I speak so that I will fearlessly make known the mystery of the gospel" (Ephesians 6:18-19). Paul's words underscore the need for constant, Spirit-led prayer in preaching. Through prayer, preachers can intercede for themselves and their congregations, seeking divine enablement and deepening their understanding and proclamation of the Gospel.

Dependence on the Holy Spirit is inseparable from prayer. The Holy Spirit is the divine agent who empowers, teaches, and illuminates the preacher's understanding of God's Word. Jesus promised the disciples that the Holy Spirit would be their Advocate, guiding them into all truth (John 16:13). The Holy Spirit equips preachers with spiritual gifts, such as teaching, wisdom, and discernment, enabling them to effectively communicate the truths of Scripture.

The apostle Paul reminds the Corinthian believers of the vital role of the Holy Spirit in preaching when he says, "My message and my preaching were not with wise and persuasive words, but with a demonstration of the Spirit's power so that your faith might not rest on human wisdom, but on God's power" (1 Corinthians 2:4-5). This passage emphasises the necessity of relying on the Holy Spirit's power rather than human eloquence or persuasive techniques. Preachers are called to yield to the leading of the Holy Spirit, trusting in His guidance and empowerment to bring about spiritual transformation in the hearers' lives.

As preachers depend on the Holy Spirit and engage in prayer, they position themselves as vessels through which God's message flows. They recognise that it is not their own wisdom or efforts that bring about transformation but the power of God working through them. Through prayer, preachers acknowledge their dependence on God and invite His intervention in every aspect of their preaching ministry.

In the next sections, we will explore practical ways to cultivate a vibrant prayer life and deepen our dependence on the Holy Spirit. We will examine the disciplines of prayer, reflection, and listening to God, as well as the role of the Holy Spirit in illuminating and applying the truths of Scripture. We will delve into the importance of seeking God's guidance through prayer and the ongoing reliance on the Holy Spirit in the sermon preparation and delivery process.

By engaging in consistent and fervent prayer, preachers open themselves up to the transformative work of God in their own lives and in the lives of their congregation. Prayer allows preachers to align their hearts with God's heart, seek His wisdom and direction, and surrender their own agendas and limitations. It is in the place of prayer that preachers can find clarity, inspiration, and empowerment to effectively communicate God's message.

Dependence on the Holy Spirit is not a mere theological concept but a practical reality that preachers are called to embrace. It involves cultivating a sensitivity to the leading and prompting of the Holy Spirit, allowing Him to guide and shape the preaching process. The Holy Spirit provides insights into the meaning and application of Scripture, empowers the preacher's words with conviction, and touches the hearts of the hearers, bringing about transformation.

Jesus promised His disciples, "But you will receive power when the Holy Spirit comes on you; and you will be my witnesses" (Acts 1:8). This promise also applies to preachers today. The Holy Spirit empowers preachers to boldly and faithfully proclaim the Gospel, enabling them to become effective witnesses of God's truth.

As preachers embrace prayer and dependence on the Holy Spirit, they position themselves to experience a deeper intimacy with God and to be conduits of His grace and truth. Through prayer, preachers tap into the divine resources, seeking divine insight, strength, and inspiration. Through dependence on the Holy Spirit, preachers recognise that their efforts alone are insufficient. Still, they can fulfil their calling with God's presence and power with excellence.

In the following sections, we will explore practical strategies for cultivating a robust prayer life, including setting aside dedicated time for prayer, engaging in various forms of prayer, and developing a posture of listening to God's voice. We will also delve into how preachers can intentionally rely on the Holy Spirit, seeking His guidance, anointing, and empowerment throughout the sermon preparation and delivery.

By embracing prayer and dependence on the Holy Spirit, preachers deepen their spiritual lives and create an atmosphere where God's presence is tangible, His truth is communicated with clarity and conviction, and lives are transformed by the power of the Gospel. May we continually seek to cultivate a vibrant prayer life and a deep dependence on the Holy Spirit as we faithfully fulfil our calling to preach the Word of God.

Exegesis and Hermeneutics

Exegesis and hermeneutics are essential components of preparing to preach. They involve carefully studying, interpreting, and understanding Scripture in its original context and applying its timeless truths to the present-day audience. By engaging in rigorous exegesis and employing sound hermeneutical principles, preachers ensure that their sermons accurately reflect the intended meaning of the biblical text and effectively communicate its relevance to the lives of the hearers.

Exegesis is interpreting a passage of Scripture by investigating its historical, cultural, and literary context. It involves examining the original language, considering the author's intention, and understanding the text within the biblical narrative. Through exegesis, preachers strive to discover the text's original meaning and grasp its significance for the original audience.

The apostle Paul encourages Timothy, his protégé in ministry, to diligently study and rightly handle the Word of Truth. He says, "Do your best to present yourself to God as approved, a worker who does not need to be ashamed and correctly handles the word of truth" (2 Timothy 2:15). This exhortation highlights the importance of careful study and accurate interpretation of Scripture to faithfully proclaim its message.

On the other hand, Hermeneutics focuses on the principles and methods used to interpret and apply Scripture. It provides guidelines for understanding the meaning of the text and bridging the historical and cultural gap between the original audience and contemporary hearers. Effective hermeneutics enable preachers to apply the timeless truths of Scripture to their congregations' specific contexts and needs.

The psalmist writes, "Your word is a lamp for my feet, a light on my path" (Psalm 119:105). This verse emphasises the illuminating and guiding role of Scripture in our lives. By employing sound hermeneutical principles, preachers can effectively illuminate the Word of God, making it relevant and applicable to their congregations' specific situations and challenges.

One important hermeneutical principle is the recognition that Scripture is a unified whole, with each part contributing to the larger narrative of God's redemptive plan. Jesus Himself affirmed the unity and authority of Scripture when He said, "Do not think that I have come to abolish the Law or the Prophets; I have not come to abolish them but to fulfil them" (Matthew 5:17). Preachers should approach Scripture holistically, understanding that the Old and New Testaments are interconnected and that the entirety of Scripture points to Christ.

Another key hermeneutical principle is the application of Scripture to the contemporary context. James challenges believers to not only be hearers of the Word but also doers of it (James 1:22). Preachers must bridge the gap between the ancient biblical world and the modern world, bringing the transformative power of Scripture into the lives of their hearers. This requires discernment, cultural sensitivity, and an understanding of the specific needs and challenges faced by the congregation.

By engaging in rigorous exegesis and employing sound hermeneutical principles, preachers ensure that their sermons are grounded in the truth of Scripture and relevant to the lives of their hearers. The process of exegesis and hermeneutics is not an end in itself but a means to faithfully communicate God's Word with clarity, accuracy, and applicability.

The following sections will explore practical strategies for engaging in effective exegesis and hermeneutics. We will discuss the importance of studying the historical and cultural context of the biblical text, analysing its literary structure and genre, and employing various tools and resources to deepen our understanding of Scripture. We will also delve into bridging the gap between the original context and the present-day audience, ensuring that the timeless truths of God's Word are communicated in a way that addresses the specific needs and challenges of the congregation.

Effective exegesis and hermeneutics enable preachers to handle the Word of God with integrity and accuracy. They ensure that the message preached is firmly rooted in the biblical text, free from personal biases or misinterpretations. By diligently studying and rightly interpreting Scripture, preachers uphold the authority and relevance of God's Word, leading to spiritual growth, transformation, and the building up of the body of Christ.

May we continually seek to grow in our proficiency in exegesis and hermeneutics, always striving to approach Scripture with humility, diligence, and a deep reverence for its authority. As we engage in this process, may the Holy Spirit guide, enlighten, and empower us to faithfully proclaim the life-transforming truths of God's Word, bringing about spiritual renewal and growth in the hearers' lives.

Understanding the Historical and Literary Context of the Text

Understanding the historical and literary context of the biblical text is crucial in preparing to preach effectively. It involves gaining insights into the passage's historical setting, cultural background, and literary genre. By delving into the context, preachers can uncover the text's original meaning and apply it accurately to the lives of the contemporary audience.

The historical context provides valuable information about the time, place, and circumstances in which the text was written. It helps preachers grasp the cultural, social, and political dynamics that shaped the biblical authors' perspectives and influenced their communication. Knowledge of historical events, customs, and practices aids in interpreting the text accurately and discerning the intended message.

For example, understanding the historical context of the Israelites' exodus from Egypt and their subsequent journey through the wilderness sheds light on the significance of God's deliverance, provision, and guidance in the book of Exodus. Recognising the historical context of the early church in Acts provides insights into the challenges faced by the apostles, the expansion of the Gospel, and the establishment of the early Christian communities.

The literary context refers to the immediate literary setting of the passage within its biblical book or section. It involves considering the preceding and following verses, chapters, or sections to understand how the passage fits into the broader narrative or argument. The literary context helps preachers avoid isolated proof-texting and ensures a comprehensive understanding of the author's intended message.

Paul's letter to the Romans offers an excellent example of the significance of understanding the literary context. Each chapter builds upon the previous ones, presenting a systematic argument regarding the righteousness of God and the salvation offered through faith in Jesus Christ. By considering the literary context, preachers can grasp the flow of Paul's thoughts and communicate the coherent message of the entire epistle.

The Bible guides the importance of understanding the historical and literary context. In 2 Timothy 2:15, Paul instructs Timothy to "correctly handle the word of truth". This admonition implies interpreting and presenting Scripture accurately, which requires a thorough understanding of the historical and literary context.

In the book of Nehemiah, we find an example of the significance of understanding the historical and cultural context. Nehemiah, upon hearing about the broken walls of Jerusalem, sought permission from the king to rebuild them (Nehemiah 1:1-2:8). Through studying the historical context of this period, we gain insights into the political dynamics and challenges faced by Nehemiah, as well as the significance of the restoration of Jerusalem's walls for the people of Israel.

By diligently studying the historical and literary context of the text, preachers can interpret the Scriptures faithfully and accurately. This understanding helps to ensure that the message preached aligns with the original intent of the biblical authors. It also enables preachers to apply the timeless truths of Scripture in a way that resonates with the contemporary audience, addressing their specific needs and challenges.

In the following sections, we will explore practical strategies for researching and understanding the historical and literary context of the biblical text. We will examine the importance of studying historical background, cultural practices, and literary genres. Through these endeavours, preachers can uncover the richness and depth of God's Word, leading to more impactful and transformative sermons.

Practical Tips for Effective Exegesis and Hermeneutical Standards

Effective exegesis and hermeneutics are crucial for accurately understanding and interpreting Scripture. Here are some practical tips to help you engage in these disciplines effectively:

1. Study the historical and cultural context: Gain a deeper understanding of the historical and cultural background in which the text was written. This includes studying the historical setting, the author's intended audience, and the cultural practices of the time. This knowledge helps to illuminate the meaning and significance of the text.

2. Use reliable study resources: Use reliable commentaries, Bible dictionaries, concordances, and other study resources to aid your interpretation. These resources provide valuable insights into the text's original language, historical context, and cultural background.

3. Engage in linguistic analysis: If possible, delve into the original languages of the Bible, such as Hebrew, Aramaic, and Greek. Study the word meanings, grammatical structures, and syntax to grasp the nuances and richness of the text. Various language study tools, lexicons, and interlinear translations can assist you.

4. Consider literary genres: Recognise the different genres present in Scripture, such as narrative, poetry, wisdom literature, prophecy, and epistles. Each genre has its unique characteristics and should be interpreted accordingly. Understanding the literary genre helps discern the author's intent and message.

5. Apply sound principles of interpretation: Familiarise yourself with established principles of interpretation, such as the grammatical-historical method, which emphasises understanding the text's grammatical and historical context. Consider the literary devices, figures of speech, and rhetorical techniques employed by the author. Interpret Scripture in light of its own internal consistency and coherence.

6. Seek the guidance of the Holy Spirit: Pray for wisdom and illumination from the Holy Spirit as you engage in exegesis and hermeneutics. Depend on the Spirit to guide you into truth and provide insights into the meaning and application of the text.

7. Consider the larger biblical context: Interpret each passage in light of the broader biblical narrative and theological themes. Scripture interprets Scripture, and understanding the interconnections between passages helps arrive at a comprehensive understanding of the message.

8. Consult trusted teachers and scholars: Engage in discussions with trusted pastors, theologians, and biblical scholars with expertise in exegesis and hermeneutics. Seek their guidance and insights to deepen your understanding of the text.

9. Apply the principles of application: Once you have grasped the meaning of the text, consider its application to your own life and the lives of others. Look for timeless truths and principles that can be applied in different contexts and situations.

10. Remain humble and open to correction: Recognise that the process of interpretation is a lifelong journey. Be open to correction and willing to refine your understanding as you continue to study and grow in your knowledge of God's Word.

By incorporating these practical tips into your study and interpretation of Scripture, you can develop a solid foundation in exegesis and hermeneutics, enabling you to accurately understand and effectively apply the message of the Bible.

The Grammatical-Historical Method of Bible Interpretation

The grammatical-historical method of interpretation is an approach to understanding Scripture that emphasises the importance of examining the biblical text's grammar, syntax, and historical context. This method seeks to uncover the original meaning and intent of the author within the cultural and historical context in which the text was written. The method aims to interpret the text faithfully by considering the grammar and historical setting, avoiding subjective or allegorical interpretations.

1. Grammar: The grammatical aspect of the method focuses on understanding the words, phrases, and sentences of the biblical text in their original languages. It involves studying the grammar, syntax, and vocabulary to discern the author's intended meaning. This includes understanding the nuances of word meanings, verb tenses, and grammatical structures. For example, in Paul's letters, a careful study of his use of the Greek verb "justified" (dikaioō) reveals his emphasis on righteousness by faith apart from works (Romans 3:28).

2. Historical Context: The method's historical aspect involves considering the text's cultural, social, and historical background. This includes studying the political climate, religious practices, and social customs when the text was written. By understanding the historical context, we gain insights into the author's intended meaning and the message's relevance to its original audience. For instance, understanding the historical context of Jesus' teachings on the Kingdom of God helps us grasp the significance of His words within the

expectations and hopes of first-century Jewish society (Matthew 4:17).

3. Authorial Intent: The grammatical-historical method seeks to uncover the author's original intent behind the text. It aims to understand what the author intended to communicate to the original audience. This approach acknowledges that the meaning of the text is not determined solely by the reader's subjective interpretation but by the author's intended message. For example, studying the cultural and historical context of the book of James helps us grasp the author's intention to address issues of faith and works in the early Christian community (James 2:14-26).

4. Contextual Consistency: The grammatical-historical method emphasises interpreting Scripture in light of its internal consistency and coherence. It considers the broader context of the passage, such as the surrounding verses, the chapter, and the entire book. This approach recognises that Scripture is a unified whole, and passages should be interpreted harmoniously with the biblical message. For instance, understanding the broader context of Jesus' teaching on love and the Greatest Commandment (Matthew 22:34-40) helps us see its alignment with the biblical theme of love for God and neighbour (Leviticus 19:18).

5. Application: The grammatical-historical method does not stop at understanding the text's original meaning but also considers its application for contemporary audiences. It recognises that the timeless truths and principles found in Scripture are relevant and applicable today. However, the method distinguishes between the original meaning and the contemporary application, avoiding allegorical or subjective interpretations. This approach allows for the relevance and transformative power of Scripture to be realised in different

contexts and cultures.

By employing the grammatical-historical method, we can approach Scripture with a commitment to understanding the original meaning intended by the authors and the historical context in which they wrote. This method helps us to navigate the complexities of interpretation, ensuring that our understanding of Scripture is grounded in a faithful and objective approach. It enables us to appreciate the richness and depth of God's Word, providing a solid foundation for sound biblical interpretation and application in our lives today.

Word Meanings, Grammatical Structures and Syntax

When preparing to preach, paying attention to word meanings, grammatical structures, and syntax is essential for grasping the nuances and richness of the Bible text. These elements provide insights into the original intent and message of the biblical passage. Here's a detailed discussion of how these aspects contribute to effective sermon preparation:

1. Word Meanings: Understanding the meanings of individual words is crucial for accurate interpretation. Words carry specific connotations, nuances, and cultural associations that shape their usage in a given context. Utilising lexicons, concordances, and word study resources helps uncover the original meaning of words in their original languages (Hebrew, Aramaic, and Greek). Exploring the root forms, semantic ranges, and related words enhances comprehension of the text's deeper layers of meaning. For example, in the Sermon on the Mount, Jesus uses the Greek word "makarios" to describe the blessedness of those who possess specific qualities (Matthew 5:3-11). Understanding the various dimensions of "makarios" enriches understanding Jesus' teachings.

2. Grammatical Structures: Examining the grammatical structures within a passage sheds light on the relationships between words, phrases, and clauses. Identifying subjects, verbs, objects, modifiers, and conjunctions clarifies the flow of thought and emphasises key ideas. Recognising the grammatical role of a word or phrase helps discern its

intended function and significance. For instance, understanding the grammatical construction of Paul's sentence in Romans 3:24-26 ("justified...through the redemption that is in Christ Jesus") highlights the inseparable link between justification and redemption in Paul's theological framework.

3. Syntax: Syntax is the arrangement and order of words and phrases in a sentence or paragraph. It encompasses sentence structure, word order, and rhetorical devices employed by biblical authors. Analysing the text's syntactical patterns and literary devices helps uncover emphasis, repetition, contrasts, comparisons, and other rhetorical strategies. This understanding enables the preacher to emphasise the intended impact of the passage on the listeners. For example, recognising the chiastic structure in the Lord's Prayer (Matthew 6:9-13) brings out the deliberate arrangement of themes and petitions, enhancing its impact when preached.

By examining word meanings, grammatical structures, and syntax, preachers can delve deeper into the nuances and richness of the Bible text. This thorough analysis aids in uncovering the author's original intent, clarifying the logical flow of thought, and emphasising key concepts. It helps preachers avoid misinterpretation or superficial understanding, enabling them to communicate the text's intended message more effectively.

This analysis assists in crafting sermons that are faithful to the text and its intended meaning. It provides a solid foundation for developing relevant and impactful illustrations, applications, and points of emphasis. By aligning the message with the text's linguistic and grammatical features, preachers can ensure that their sermons accurately convey the biblical truth to the congregation.

However, it is essential to balance scholarly analysis and practical application. The goal is not simply to impress with technical knowledge but to communicate God's message in a way that engages the hearts and minds of the listeners. While thorough exegesis is vital, it should ultimately serve the purpose of faithfully presenting the truth of God's Word in a way that speaks to the needs and context of the congregation.

Dictionaries, Concordances and other tools

Dictionaries, concordances, and other tools in sermon preparation are very important for preachers. These resources provide valuable insights into biblical texts' meaning, context, and nuances, enabling preachers to deepen their understanding and effectively communicate the message to their congregations. Here are some key reasons why these tools are essential:

1. Word Meaning and Context: Dictionaries are invaluable in exploring the meaning of words in their original languages. They provide definitions, etymology, and various shades of meaning, helping preachers grasp the depth and richness of biblical vocabulary. Understanding the original meaning of a word can shed light on the author's intended message and prevent misinterpretation.

2. Cultural and Historical Context: Biblical concordances and commentaries offer historical and cultural context, providing background information on customs, traditions, and historical events. This knowledge helps preachers bridge the gap between the ancient biblical world and the contemporary audience, making the message more relevant and relatable.

3. Cross-Referencing and Comparative Study: Tools like concordances enable preachers to locate related passages and compare biblical texts. This practice helps establish connections, uncover recurring themes, and gain a broader perspective on a particular topic or passage. By cross-referencing and conducting comparative studies, preachers can ensure a comprehensive understanding of the biblical

message.

4. Interpretive Guidance: Commentaries and theological resources provide valuable interpretive guidance from experienced scholars. They offer different perspectives, theological insights, and historical interpretations, helping preachers navigate complex passages and challenging theological concepts. These resources can assist in avoiding doctrinal errors and ensuring sound biblical teaching.

5. Language and Syntax: Understanding biblical texts' grammatical structure and syntax is vital for accurate interpretation. Tools like grammar and lexicons aid in analysing sentence structure, verb tenses, and grammatical relationships, enabling preachers to precisely interpret the text and convey its intended meaning.

6. Contextual Application: Resources such as study Bibles and sermon illustrations provide practical applications of biblical truths to contemporary life. They offer examples, anecdotes, and real-life stories that illustrate the relevance and impact of the message. Incorporating contextual application enhances the sermon's practicality. It enables the congregation to see how biblical truths relate to their lives.

7. Clarity and Accuracy: Preparing a sermon requires attention to detail and accuracy. Utilising dictionaries, concordances, and other tools ensures that preachers accurately interpret and communicate the biblical message. It helps avoid misinterpretation, misleading statements, or incomplete understanding, leading to a clear and accurate presentation of God's Word.

Using dictionaries, concordances, and other tools in sermon preparation enhances the preacher's knowledge, enriches their understanding of Scripture, and strengthens the impact of their sermons. By employing these resources, preachers can delve deeper into the biblical text, convey its intended message accurately, and engage their congregation with a well-informed and transformative proclamation of God's Word.

3. Planning the Preaching Series

Planning a preaching series is an essential step in effective sermon preparation. Rather than randomly selecting passages or topics each week, a well-designed preaching series provides coherence, continuity, and depth to the messages delivered to the congregation. It allows preachers to explore specific themes, biblical books, or theological concepts over a series of sermons, providing a comprehensive and cohesive learning experience for the church community.

In this section, we will delve into planning a preaching series. We will explore the factors to consider when determining the scope of the series, selecting the texts to preach, and establishing the order and structure of the sermons. By carefully planning the preaching series, preachers can cultivate a rich and meaningful journey through God's Word, guiding the congregation toward spiritual growth, understanding, and application.

Determining the Scope of the Series: When embarking on a preaching series, it is crucial to define its scope. This involves clarifying the series' purpose, duration, and overarching theme. Preachers may focus on a particular book of the Bible, a specific theological topic, a season of the liturgical calendar, or a practical aspect of Christian living. By establishing the scope, preachers provide a clear framework to craft their sermons, ensuring a unified and purposeful series.

Choosing the Texts to Preach: Once the scope is defined, the next step is selecting the texts to be preached. This requires carefully considering the biblical passages aligning with the series' theme and supporting its objectives. Preachers may preach through a specific book or section of

Scripture, explore related passages from different parts of the Bible, or follow a thematic approach that draws from various biblical texts. The selection of texts should be guided by a desire to present a comprehensive and balanced view of God's Word.

Order and Structure of the Series: The order and structure of the preaching series play a vital role in its effectiveness. Preachers must determine the logical progression of the sermons, considering how the selected texts build upon and relate to one another. They may follow a chronological or thematic order, arrange the sermons around specific concepts or principles, or adopt a narrative approach that tells a cohesive story throughout the series. The structure should facilitate the congregation's understanding, engagement, and retention of the preached messages.

A well-planned preaching series offers numerous benefits. It provides a coherent and focused learning experience for the congregation, allowing for a deeper exploration of biblical truths. It also enables preachers to address specific theological, spiritual, or practical issues over a series of sermons, providing a more comprehensive understanding and application of the Word of God. A well-structured series enhances the anticipation and participation of the congregation, fostering a sense of unity and shared spiritual growth.

The following sections will delve into practical strategies for planning a preaching series. We will explore methods for defining the scope, selecting texts, and organising the sermons effectively. By engaging in thoughtful planning, preachers can guide their congregation on a transformative journey through God's Word, nurturing their faith and equipping them for faithful living.

May planning a preaching series be a source of inspiration, creativity, and spiritual growth for preachers and congregations. As we embark on this journey together, let us seek the guidance of the Holy Spirit, relying on His wisdom and insight to shape the preaching series into a powerful tool for proclaiming the Gospel and edifying the body of Christ.

Determining the Scope of the Series

Determining the scope of a preaching series is an important step in planning and organising impactful sermons. It involves defining the purpose, duration, and overarching theme of the series, setting the foundation for a cohesive and focused exploration of God's Word. By carefully considering these factors, preachers can guide the congregation on a meaningful spiritual growth and understanding journey.

1. Defining the Purpose: The first consideration in determining the scope of a preaching series is to clarify its purpose. What do you hope to achieve through this series? Are you aiming to provide a comprehensive study of a specific book of the Bible? Do you want to address a particular theological topic or challenge facing the congregation? Are you seeking to explore a practical aspect of Christian living? By defining the purpose, you establish the primary objective of the series and align it with the needs and goals of the congregation.

2. Setting the Duration: The next step is determining the series' duration once the purpose is established. Will it span a few weeks, a few months, or an entire season? Consider the depth of the topic or book being covered, as well as the attention span and engagement of the congregation. A shorter series may provide a focused study on a specific aspect. In comparison, a longer series allows for a more comprehensive exploration. Setting the duration helps manage expectations and allows for effective planning and pacing of the sermons.

3. Establishing the Overarching Theme: The series' overarching theme serves as a unifying thread that runs through all the

sermons. It provides cohesion and coherence to the messages, allowing the congregation to grasp the central message and purpose of the series. The theme can be derived from the chosen book of the Bible, a theological concept, or a practical theme relevant to the congregation's needs. By establishing a clear theme, preachers create a framework for developing and connecting the sermons.

For example, suppose the series' purpose is to explore the book of Ephesians. In that case, the scope might be defined as a comprehensive study of this letter written by the apostle Paul. The duration could span several months to allow for an in-depth examination of the rich theological teachings found in Ephesians. The overarching theme might be "The Church: God's Plan for Unity and Transformation," emphasising the importance of unity in Christ and the transformative power of the Gospel in the life of the believer and the church.

Biblical wisdom encourages us to intentionally set the scope and purpose of our teaching. In 2 Timothy 3:16-17, we read, "All Scripture is breathed out by God and profitable for teaching, for reproof, for correction, and for training in righteousness, that the man of God may be complete, equipped for every good work" (ESV). This reminds us of the significance of studying and proclaiming the entirety of God's Word, ensuring that our preaching series encompasses the breadth and depth of Scripture.

By defining a preaching series's purpose, duration, and overarching theme, preachers can provide a focused and transformative experience for the congregation. This intentional approach allows for a comprehensive exploration of biblical truths, addressing the community's needs, challenges, and spiritual growth. It enables preachers to guide their congregation on a coherent and purposeful journey through God's Word, illuminating the richness and relevance of Scripture for their lives.

In the subsequent sections, we will explore practical strategies for selecting texts, organising sermons, and crafting an effective preaching series. Through careful planning and thoughtful execution, preachers can create a meaningful and impactful series that fosters spiritual growth, deepens understanding, and cultivates a vibrant faith in the hearts and minds of the congregation.

Choosing the Texts to Preach

Once the scope of the preaching series has been defined, the next step is to carefully select the texts to be preached. The choice of biblical passages plays a crucial role in shaping the series' content, flow, and message. By thoughtfully selecting texts that align with the overarching theme and purpose of the series, preachers can provide a well-rounded and comprehensive exploration of God's Word.

1. Alignment with the Series Theme: When choosing texts for a preaching series, it is essential to ensure that they align with the overarching theme established for the series. The selected passages should contribute to the central message and purpose of the series. They should shed light on the theme, provide different perspectives or insights, and reinforce the main ideas being communicated. By maintaining this alignment, preachers create a cohesive and unified series that deepens the understanding and application of the chosen theme.

2. Biblical Variety and Balance: A well-planned preaching series should aim to provide a balance of biblical variety. This means selecting texts from different genres (such as narratives, epistles, poetry, and prophetic literature) and different sections of the Bible (Old Testament and New Testament). By incorporating a diverse range of biblical texts, preachers expose the congregation to the breadth and depth of God's Word, ensuring a comprehensive exploration of its teachings. It prevents overemphasis on certain passages or themes while neglecting others.

3. Complementing and Expanding on Previous Sermons: If the preaching series continues previous sermons or builds upon a

specific biblical book or topic, selecting texts complementing and expanding on what has been previously taught is important. This creates a sense of continuity and progression in the series, allowing for deeper exploration and understanding of the chosen subject matter. By selecting texts that build upon previous sermons, preachers provide a cohesive and enriching learning experience for the congregation.

4. Practical Application and Relevance: Preachers should consider their practical application and relevance to the congregation's lives when selecting texts. The chosen passages should convey theological truths and offer practical insights and guidance for Christian living. By including texts that address the congregation's needs, challenges, and spiritual growth, preachers ensure that the series has a meaningful impact on their daily lives. This fosters a connection between the biblical message and its application in contemporary contexts.

The process of selecting texts requires careful discernment and prayerful consideration. It involves studying the Bible to seek God's guidance and wisdom. In James 1:5, we are encouraged, "If any of you lacks wisdom, let him ask God, who gives generously to all without reproach, and it will be given him" (ESV). By relying on God's wisdom and guidance, preachers can make informed and inspired choices in selecting the texts shaping the preaching series.

Prepreachers can create a rich and impactful preaching series by choosing texts that align with the series theme, provide biblical variety and balance, complement previous sermons, and offer practical application. Through carefully selecting texts, they guide the congregation on a transformative journey through Scripture, deepening their understanding of God's Word and its relevance to their lives.

In the subsequent sections, we will explore practical methods for organising the selected texts within the preaching series. We will discuss the order and structure of the sermons, ensuring a logical progression and coherence that enhances the congregation's learning experience. With thoughtful selection and organisation of texts, preachers can present a comprehensive and inspiring series that illuminates the timeless truths of Scripture and encourages spiritual growth in the hearts and minds of the congregation.

Order and Structure of the Series

The order and structure of a preaching series are crucial for its effectiveness in conveying the intended message and facilitating the congregation's understanding and engagement. By carefully considering the arrangement and flow of the sermons, preachers can create a logical progression that enhances the coherence and impact of the series. The order and structure allow for the development of themes, connections between passages, and the effective communication of God's Word.

1. Logical Progression: One important aspect of planning a preaching series is determining the logical progression of the sermons. The sermons should build upon one another, leading the congregation on a journey of understanding and discovery. Preachers can consider various approaches when establishing this progression. They may choose a chronological approach, following the biblical narrative or the order in which the books were written. Alternatively, they may opt for a thematic approach, organising the sermons around specific concepts or principles. The key is to ensure that each sermon flows naturally from the previous one, providing a sense of continuity and allowing for a deeper exploration of the chosen theme.

2. Cohesive Connection between Passages: In a preaching series, it is essential to establish cohesive connections between the selected passages. These connections can be based on themes, motifs, theological concepts, or narrative elements. By identifying and highlighting these connections, preachers help the congregation see the unity and interrelatedness of

God's Word. They demonstrate how different passages and books of the Bible contribute to a comprehensive understanding of the chosen theme. This interconnectedness enriches the congregation's comprehension of Scripture and fosters a holistic view of God's revelation.

3. Balancing Depth and Variety: While maintaining a logical progression and cohesive connection, preachers should also strive to balance the depth and variety of the sermons within the series. Some passages may require more in-depth exploration and exposition, allowing for a comprehensive text study. Others may provide opportunities for broader themes, practical applications, or contrasting perspectives. By incorporating a mix of depth and variety, preachers cater to the congregation's diverse needs and learning styles, ensuring a well-rounded and engaging series.

4. Introduction and Conclusion: Within the structure of the series, preachers should pay attention to the introduction and conclusion of each sermon. The introduction sets the stage, capturing the congregation's attention and providing context for exploring the passage. It establishes the relevance and significance of the sermon, drawing the listeners into the message. The conclusion summarises the main points, reinforces the key takeaways, and provides the congregation with a call to action or reflection. Well-crafted introductions and conclusions enhance the overall impact of each sermon and contribute to the coherence of the series.

When considering the order and structure of a preaching series, preachers can seek inspiration and guidance from the Bible itself. In Psalm 119:18, the psalmist prays, "Open my eyes, that I may behold wondrous things out of your law" (ESV). By approaching the Scriptures with a humble and open heart, preachers can discern the divine wisdom and inspiration that informs the structure and arrangement of the biblical texts. They can draw insights from narrative arcs, thematic progressions, and rhetorical techniques employed in the Bible to create a compelling and impactful series structure.

By carefully organising the sermons within a preaching series, preachers provide a coherent and engaging learning experience for the congregation. The logical progression, cohesive connections between passages, the balance of depth and variety, and well-crafted introductions and conclusions all contribute to the effectiveness of the series. Through thoughtful planning and attention to structure, preachers guide the congregation on a transformative journey through God's Word, enabling them to deepen their understanding, apply biblical truths, and grow in their faith.

Practical Tips for Crafting a Sermon

Crafting a sermon requires careful planning and preparation to effectively communicate the message of God's Word. Here are some practical tips to consider when crafting a sermon:

1. Start with Prayer: Seek God's guidance and inspiration as you begin the sermon preparation process. Pray for wisdom, clarity, and sensitivity to the leading of the Holy Spirit. Jesus reminds us in John 15:5, "I am the vine; you are the branches. If you remain in me and I in you, you will bear much fruit; apart from me, you can do nothing."

2. Understand the Text: Engage in a thorough exegesis of the biblical passage. Study the context, consider the author's intended message, and grasp the main themes and key points. Use tools such as commentaries, Bible dictionaries, and concordances to better understand the text. Remember Paul's exhortation to Timothy in 2 Timothy 2:15, "Do your best to present yourself to God as one approved, a worker who does not need to be ashamed and who correctly handles the word of truth."

3. Identify the Central Message: Determine the passage's main message or central idea. Focus on the primary message that the text conveys and ensure that your sermon centres around it. Look for key themes, principles, or calls to action that resonate with the intended audience. Consider the example of the Apostle Peter in Acts 2:14-41, where he delivers a powerful sermon on the day of Pentecost, emphasising the fulfilment of Old Testament prophecies through Jesus Christ.

4. Develop a Clear Structure: Organise your sermon clearly and

logically. Consider using an outline or structure that helps your listeners follow the flow of your message. This can include an introduction that captures attention, body points supporting the main message, and a conclusion summarising and challenging the audience. Paul's approach in 1 Corinthians 15:1-8 provides a structured presentation of the Gospel message, highlighting Christ's death, burial, resurrection, and appearances to various witnesses.

5. Use Illustrations and Examples: Incorporate relatable illustrations, stories, and examples to make the message more engaging and applicable to the listeners' lives. Jesus frequently used parables to teach spiritual truths in a way that people could understand and relate to. Look for relevant anecdotes, real-life scenarios, or biblical narratives that bring the message to life and resonate with the congregation.

6. Provide Application: Help your listeners understand how biblical truth applies to their lives. Offer practical steps, challenges, or insights, encouraging them to live out the message in their daily walk with Christ. James emphasises the importance of applying God's Word in James 1:22, saying, "Do not merely listen to the word, and so deceive yourselves. Do what it says."

7. Use Clear and Engaging Language: Communicate clearly, simply, and authentically. Use language that is appropriate for your audience and avoids unnecessary jargon. Vary your tone, pace, and volume to maintain interest and engagement. Consider the Apostle Paul's instruction in Colossians 4:6, "Let your conversation be always full of grace, seasoned with salt, so that you may know how to answer everyone."

8. Practice and Seek Feedback: Practice delivering your sermon aloud to ensure smooth delivery and timing. Seek feedback from trusted individuals who can provide constructive

criticism and help you improve. Embrace a posture of humility and a desire for continuous growth in your preaching ministry.

Remember that crafting a sermon is not merely an intellectual exercise but a spiritual endeavour. Allow the Holy Spirit to guide and shape your preparation process, trusting that God will use your faithful efforts to impact the lives of those who hear His Word.

As Paul reminds us in 1 Corinthians 2:4-5, "My message and my preaching were not with wise and persuasive words, but with a demonstration of the Spirit's power so that your faith might not rest on human wisdom, but on God's power." Ultimately, the effectiveness of your sermon lies in the power of the Holy Spirit working through you.

Crafting a sermon requires diligent study, prayerful reflection, and intentional communication. By understanding the text, identifying the central message, employing clear structure, using illustrations and examples, providing practical application, using engaging language, and seeking feedback, you can deliver a sermon that effectively communicates God's Word and impacts the hearts and lives of your listeners. Remember, the ultimate goal is to glorify God, edify the church, and equip believers to live out their faith in the world.

4. Crafting the Sermon

Crafting a sermon is a skilful art that requires careful thought, preparation, and attention to detail. It is the process of shaping and delivering a message that effectively communicates God's Word, engages the congregation, and facilitates spiritual transformation. The sermon is a vital medium through which preachers can convey biblical truths and inspire, challenge, and encourage the listeners. This section will delve into the various elements of crafting an impactful and edifying sermon.

1. Developing the Theme and Purpose of the Sermon: Every sermon should have a clear theme and purpose. The theme serves as the central focus or main idea of the message. At the same time, the purpose identifies the specific intention or desired outcome of the sermon. The theme and purpose should be derived from the preached biblical text and aligned with the overall theme of the preaching series. By carefully developing the theme and purpose, preachers ensure that their sermons have a clear direction and effectively communicate the intended message.

2. Outlining the Sermon: An outline serves as a roadmap for the sermon, guiding the preacher in organising the content and flow of the message. It provides a logical structure and helps maintain a coherent progression of ideas. The outline typically includes an introduction, main points, supporting subpoints, and a conclusion. Each section of the outline should be concise, well-structured, and support the overall theme and purpose of the sermon. An effective outline enables the preacher to deliver the message in a structured and organised

manner, making it easier for the congregation to follow along and grasp the key points.

3. Introduction and Conclusion: A sermon's introduction and conclusion are critical as they frame and reinforce the main message. The introduction should capture the congregation's attention, create anticipation, and establish the context for the sermon. It can include personal anecdotes, relevant illustrations, or thought-provoking questions to engage the listeners. Conversely, the conclusion summarises the main points, reinforces the key message, and provides the congregation with a clear call to action or reflection. Well-crafted introductions and conclusions leave a lasting impact and help the congregation connect with the sermon's central ideas.

4. Illustrations and Application: Illustrations bring the sermon to life and make it relatable to the congregation's everyday experiences. Illustrations can be stories, examples, anecdotes, or visual aids that help clarify and reinforce the sermon's main points. They serve to capture attention, provide context, and enhance understanding. Application, on the other hand, bridges the gap between biblical truths and practical relevance. It demonstrates how the biblical message applies to the listeners' lives and guides their spiritual growth and transformation. Well-chosen illustrations and relevant applications help the congregation connect with the sermon's message on a personal level.

Crafting a sermon is a sacred task that requires the study of God's Word and a deep understanding of the congregation's needs. It is an opportunity for preachers to faithfully communicate the timeless truths of Scripture and guide the listeners towards a closer relationship with God. In the subsequent sections, we will explore each element of sermon crafting in more detail, providing practical strategies and insights for developing impactful and transformational messages. By honing their sermon preparation and delivery skills, preachers can effectively proclaim God's Word, edify the congregation, and inspire them to live meaningfully.

Developing the Theme and Purpose of the Sermon

Developing a clear theme and purpose for a sermon is essential for effective communication and impactful preaching. The theme serves as the central idea or focus of the message. At the same time, the purpose identifies the specific intention or desired outcome. A well-developed theme and purpose ensure the sermon has a clear direction, coherence, and relevance to the congregation.

1. Theme: The theme of a sermon should be derived from the biblical text being preached and aligned with the overall theme of the preaching series, if applicable. It should capture the essence of the passage and convey its main message or theological truth. The theme provides a unifying thread that connects various sermon elements, such as the main points, illustrations, and application.

Preachers should thoroughly study and interpret the selected biblical passage to develop the theme. They should consider the text's context, literary genre, historical background, and theological significance. By immersing themselves in the Scriptures, preachers can discern the central message and identify emerging themes and ideas.

For example, if preaching from the Gospel of John, a possible theme could be "The Deity and Humanity of Jesus Christ." This theme captures the central focus of John's Gospel, which emphasises the divinity of Jesus while highlighting His humanity and the significance of His redemptive work.

1. Purpose: The purpose of a sermon goes beyond the theme

and delves into the specific intention or desired outcome of the message. It answers the question, "What do I want the congregation to understand, experience, or do as a result of this sermon?" The purpose shapes the sermon's content, tone, and application.

The purpose can vary depending on the specific needs of the congregation. It may include fostering spiritual growth, providing comfort and encouragement, challenging complacency, promoting repentance and transformation, or equipping the listeners for faithful living. The purpose should be rooted in the biblical text and reflect the heart of God's Word.

For instance, the purpose of a sermon on the theme mentioned earlier, "The Deity and Humanity of Jesus Christ," could be to deepen the congregation's understanding of the person and work of Jesus Christ, leading to a renewed sense of awe, worship, and commitment to follow Him.

1. Biblical Foundation: Developing the theme and purpose of a sermon requires a solid biblical foundation. It is essential to ensure that the theme and purpose align with the teachings of Scripture and accurately reflect the message of the selected passage. By grounding the sermon in the Word of God, preachers convey the authority and relevance of God's truth to the congregation.

The Bible provides guidance for developing the theme and purpose of a sermon. In 2 Timothy 3:16-17, it is stated, "All Scripture is breathed out by God and profitable for teaching, for reproof, for correction, and for training in righteousness, that the man of God may be complete, equipped for every good work" (ESV). This passage emphasises the transformative power of Scripture and its ability to equip believers for faithful living. Preachers can draw inspiration and direction from the biblical text as they develop the theme and purpose, knowing that the Word of God is sufficient and authoritative.

Preachers provide a solid sermon foundation by developing a clear theme and purpose. The theme captures the central idea of the passage, while the purpose identifies the desired outcome for the congregation. The theme and purpose should be rooted in careful biblical study and interpretation. They serve as guiding principles in crafting the sermon's content, structure, and delivery, ensuring that it effectively communicates God's Word and brings about spiritual transformation in the listeners' lives.

Outlining the Sermon

Outlining a sermon is a vital step in sermon preparation. It helps preachers organise their thoughts, structure their message, and maintain a logical flow of ideas. An outline is a roadmap that guides the preacher in delivering a coherent and well-structured sermon. It provides a framework for the sermon's main points, subpoints, supporting Scripture, illustrations, and application.

1. Introduction to Outlining: An outline is the backbone of a sermon, ensuring that the preacher stays focused on the main theme and purpose. It helps preachers avoid rambling or disjointed presentations and allows for a clear and organised delivery. Outlining is not meant to restrict creativity or spontaneity but to provide a structured framework that enhances clarity and comprehension.

2. Components of an Outline: An effective outline typically consists of several key components:

a. Introduction: The introduction section of the outline sets the stage for the sermon. It aims to capture the congregation's attention, create interest, and provide an overview of the sermon's content. The introduction may include a compelling story, a relevant quote, or a thought-provoking question that engages the listeners from the beginning.

b. Main Points: The main points of the sermon outline represent the key ideas or concepts that support the sermon's theme and purpose. These points should be derived directly from the biblical text and reflect the conveyed central teachings or truths. Each main point should be concise, clear, and specific, allowing the preacher to develop them further during the sermon.

c. Subpoints: Subpoints provide additional depth and support to the main points. They serve as subcategories or aspects related to each main point. Subpoints help the preacher provide comprehensive explanations, examples, or illustrations illuminating the main ideas.

d. Supporting Scripture: Including supporting Scripture references within the outline is essential for grounding the sermon in God's Word. Relevant passages that support and reinforce the main points and subpoints should be included. By incorporating specific verses or passages, preachers demonstrate the biblical basis for their message and allow the Scriptures to speak directly to the congregation.

e. Illustrations and Application: Integrating illustrations and application within the outline helps bring the sermon to life and make it relevant to the listeners. Illustrations can be personal anecdotes, stories, or examples that clarify or emphasise the main points. The application involves showing how the biblical truths presented in the sermon can be applied to the everyday lives of the congregation, fostering personal growth and transformation.

1. Biblical Precedence for Outlining: The practice of outlining sermons finds biblical precedence in the structure and organisation of many biblical texts. For instance, the apostle Paul often presented his teachings in a structured and organised manner. In his epistles, Paul used outlines to present his theological arguments and practical instructions. One notable example is Romans 5:12-21, where Paul presents a logical and well-structured argument about the impact of Adam's sin and the gift of God's grace through Jesus Christ.

The book of Proverbs provides wisdom literature in a concise and structured form, with various proverbs organised thematically or categorically. The Psalms also exhibit a degree of structure, with many psalms following a pattern of introduction, body, and conclusion.

By using outlines, preachers follow in the footsteps of biblical authors, employing a structured approach to effectively convey their message and engage the congregation.

Outlining a sermon gives preachers a clear roadmap for delivering a coherent and well-organised message. It ensures that the sermon stays focused on the main theme and purpose while allowing flexibility for creativity and spontaneity. By including components such as the introduction, main points, subpoints, supporting Scripture, illustrations, and application, preachers can effectively communicate biblical truths and engage the congregation meaningfully.

When preachers outline their sermons, they demonstrate a commitment to diligent study and preparation, allowing the message to flow smoothly and coherently. The outline serves as a guide, helping preachers stay on track and deliver the sermon logically, making it easier for the congregation to follow along and grasp the main ideas.

While outlining a sermon, preachers should remember that the goal is not merely to convey information but to facilitate transformation. The outline should reflect the intended impact on the listeners, guiding them towards a deeper understanding of God's Word and prompting them to respond with faith and obedience.

One biblical example that highlights the importance of structure and organisation in communicating God's message is found in Nehemiah 8:1-8. When Ezra, the scribe, read from the Book of the Law to the assembled people, he did so with a well-structured approach. He stood on a platform, opened the book, and read from it, providing a clear structure for the reading. Levites were present to help the people understand the Law, indicating a deliberate effort to ensure comprehension and application.

Preachers can emulate this intentionality in delivering their sermons by using an outline. The outline enables them to communicate with clarity and purpose, allowing the congregation to receive and apply the Word of God more effectively.

Outlining a sermon is a valuable practice that helps preachers organise their thoughts, maintain a logical flow, and effectively communicate God's Word. It provides structure and coherence to the sermon, clearly conveying the theme and purpose. By incorporating components such as the introduction, main points, subpoints, supporting Scripture, illustrations, and application, preachers can deliver engaging and impactful sermons that lead to transformation in the listeners' lives. Through careful outlining, preachers honour the biblical precedent of structure and organisation in delivering God's message with clarity, relevance, and power.

Introduction and Conclusion

The introduction and conclusion of a sermon play crucial roles in capturing the congregation's attention, setting the tone for the message, and leaving a lasting impact. These sections serve as bookends that frame the sermon and provide a sense of coherence and closure. The introduction engages the listeners from the beginning. At the same time, the conclusion brings the sermon to a meaningful conclusion and encourages application.

1. Introduction: The introduction serves as the entry point into the sermon, capturing the attention and interest of the congregation. It should be carefully crafted to create anticipation and draw the listeners into the message. An effective introduction can take various forms, such as a compelling story, a thought-provoking question, a relevant anecdote, or a startling fact. The primary purpose of the introduction is to establish a connection with the listeners and establish the relevance and significance of the topic.

Preachers can draw inspiration from biblical examples that employ engaging openings in crafting the introduction. For instance, Jesus often used attention-grabbing statements, parables, or challenging questions to captivate His audience. In Luke 10:25-37, Jesus begins the Parable of the Good Samaritan with a thought-provoking question a lawyer asks: "Who is my neighbour?" This question immediately engages the listeners and sets the stage for a powerful teaching on loving one's neighbour.

1. Conclusion: The conclusion serves as the culmination of the

sermon, wrapping up the main points and leaving the congregation with a lasting impression. It provides closure and reinforces the central message, leaving the listeners with a clear takeaway or call to action. A well-crafted conclusion can inspire and challenge the congregation to apply the sermon's truths to their lives.

In the Bible, we find examples of impactful conclusions that leave a lasting impact on the hearers. In Acts 2:37-38, after Peter's sermon on the day of Pentecost, the listeners were deeply convicted and asked, "Brothers, what shall we do?" Peter's response in verse 38 serves as a powerful conclusion, urging them to repent and be baptised for the forgiveness of their sins. This conclusion prompts a significant response from the audience, demonstrating the effectiveness of a compelling and impactful conclusion.

1. Elements of Effective Introduction and Conclusion: To ensure the introduction and conclusion are effective, several elements can be incorporated:

- Clear and concise summary: The introduction and conclusion should provide a clear and concise summary of the sermon's main points. This helps the congregation grasp the overall message and reinforces key takeaways.
- Emotional connection: Both sections should establish an emotional connection with the listeners. This can be achieved through storytelling, personal experiences, or relatable examples that evoke empathy, conviction, or inspiration.
- Transition: The conclusion should provide a smooth transition from the body of the sermon to the closing remarks. It should signal the imminent end of the message and prepare the listeners for the conclusion.
- Call to action: The conclusion should include a specific and

practical call to action that encourages the congregation to apply the sermon's message daily. This can involve challenges, commitments, or steps of obedience that prompt listeners to respond.

By carefully crafting the introduction and conclusion, preachers can maximise the impact of their sermons. These sections set the stage for attentive listening and provide a memorable conclusion that inspires change and transformation. Biblical examples and principles guide the creation of engaging and impactful introductions and conclusions that connect with the congregation's hearts and minds.

Illustrations and Application

Illustrations and application are essential elements of a sermon that bring the message to life, make it relatable, and facilitate personal application. These components help bridge the gap between the biblical text and the everyday lives of the congregation, enabling them to understand and apply God's Word in practical ways.

1. Illustrations: Illustrations are examples, stories, or anecdotes that clarify and reinforce the sermon's main points. They provide tangible, relatable illustrations that help listeners grasp abstract concepts or complex ideas. Effective illustrations capture the congregation's attention, engage their emotions, and make the sermon memorable.

Biblical illustrations can be drawn from various sources. The Bible contains numerous stories, parables, and narratives that can be used as illustrations to convey spiritual truths. Jesus, the Master Teacher, frequently used parables to illustrate profound spiritual realities in a way that the common people could understand. For example, in the parable of the prodigal son (Luke 15:11-32), Jesus uses a compelling story of a wayward son and a compassionate father to depict God's unconditional love and forgiveness.

In addition to biblical illustrations, preachers can also draw from personal experiences, historical events, cultural references, or current events to provide relevant and impactful illustrations. These illustrations help connect the timeless truths of Scripture with the realities of the present-day lives of the congregation.

1. Application: Application is the process of connecting the

biblical truths presented in the sermon to the practical lives of the listeners. It shows how the sermon's message applies to their circumstances, challenges, and decisions. The effective application helps the congregation understand the relevance and significance of the sermon in their daily lives and encourages them to live out the truths they have learned.

The apostle James emphasises the importance of applying God's Word in James 1:22-25: "But be doers of the word, and not hearers only, deceiving yourselves." He urges believers not to be passive listeners but active doers of the Word. The application transforms biblical knowledge into transformative action, producing spiritual growth and maturity.

The application can take various forms, such as:

- Personal application: Encouraging individuals to examine their own lives and identify areas where they need to align their thoughts, attitudes, and actions with God's Word.
- Practical application: Providing specific steps or actions that individuals can take to live out the principles and teachings of the sermon. This may involve changing relationships, habits, priorities, or decision-making processes.
- Relational application: Highlighting the implications of the sermon for relationships within families, communities, workplaces, and the broader society. This can involve promoting forgiveness, reconciliation, love, and justice.
- Missional Application: Challenging believers to apply the sermon's message in evangelistic efforts, disciple-making, or involvement in social justice initiatives. It calls for actively living out the Gospel in a way that impacts and transforms the world around them.

Effective illustrations and application work together to make the sermon relatable, memorable, and actionable. They help the congregation connect with the message personally, fostering deeper understanding, conviction, and transformation. By combining biblical examples, personal experiences, and cultural references, preachers can bring the sermon to life and inspire the congregation to live out the truths of God's Word in their daily lives.

5. Delivering the Sermon

Effective sermon delivery is a vital aspect of preaching that goes beyond the preparation and content of the message. It involves communication, engaging the congregation, and effectively conveying God's Word in a way that captures their attention, stirs their hearts, and leads to transformation. This section will explore the various elements and skills involved in delivering a sermon, including clear communication, body language, vocal delivery, engaging the congregation, and managing nerves and distractions.

Delivering a sermon is more than just speaking words from a pulpit. It requires intentional and skilful communication that brings the message to life and makes it relevant to the listeners. A well-delivered sermon can captivate the congregation, help them connect with the truth being presented, and inspire them to respond in faith and obedience.

Throughout the Bible, we find examples of effective communicators who skillfully delivered God's messages to the people. Moses, for instance, had a unique communication style that engaged the Israelites' intellect and emotions. In Deuteronomy 32:1-4, Moses delivers a powerful poetic song declaring God's faithfulness, justice, and love. His words resonate with the listeners, evoking a response of reverence and commitment.

Similarly, the apostle Paul demonstrated effective communication skills in his letters and sermons. In Acts 17:22-31, Paul delivers a masterful sermon to the Athenians, carefully addressing their culture and worldview while proclaiming the truth of the Gospel. He engages the listeners through rhetorical questions, relevant references to their religious practices, and a clear presentation of Jesus' resurrection. His communication style demonstrates sensitivity to his audience and a deep understanding of their context.

In today's context, preachers face the challenge of communicating God's Word in a world filled with distractions and diverse communication preferences. Effective sermon delivery requires adapting to these challenges while staying true to the timeless truths of Scripture. Preachers must engage the congregation with clarity, authenticity, and relevance, ensuring that the message transcends the pulpit and resonates with the listeners' daily lives.

In the following sections, we will explore the key components of sermon delivery. We will discuss the importance of clear and effective communication, the significance of body language and vocal delivery, strategies for engaging the congregation, and practical techniques for managing nerves and distractions. By understanding and honing these skills, preachers can enhance their ability to deliver sermons that have a lasting impact on the hearts and minds of the congregation.

Sermon delivery is an art that requires both careful preparation and the guidance of the Holy Spirit. As we delve into the details of this section, let us seek to develop the skills necessary to effectively deliver God's Word, knowing that how we present the message can significantly influence its reception and impact.

Communicating Clearly and Effectively

Clear and effective communication is a fundamental aspect of delivering a sermon. It involves conveying the message in a way that is easily understood by the congregation, facilitating comprehension, engagement, and application. When preachers communicate with clarity and effectiveness, they remove barriers to understanding and enable the Word of God to penetrate the hearts and minds of the listeners.

1. Clarity of Language: Using clear and concise language is essential for effective sermon communication. Preachers should avoid jargon, technical terms, or convoluted language that may confuse or alienate the congregation. Instead, they should strive to communicate in a way accessible to people of various backgrounds, education levels, and ages. This doesn't mean compromising the depth or richness of the message but rather presenting it in a manner that can be readily grasped.

Jesus exemplified clarity in His communication. He often used simple, everyday language and relatable illustrations to convey profound spiritual truths. Mark 4:33-34 says of Jesus, "With many similar parables Jesus spoke the word to them, as much as they could understand. He did not say anything to them without using a parable." Jesus made abstract concepts tangible and relatable using parables, ensuring His audience could understand and remember the message.

1. Structured Organisation: A well-organised sermon enhances clarity and comprehension. It allows the congregation to follow the flow of thought and connect the presented points.

Preachers should employ a logical and coherent structure that guides the listeners through the sermon's progression.

One effective organisational approach is the use of main points and subpoints. Clearly articulating the main ideas and supporting them with relevant subpoints aids in the congregation's understanding and retention of the message. This approach can be seen in Paul's letters, where he often presents a clear structure with main arguments and supporting evidence.

For example, in Romans 3:21-26, Paul presents the central theme of justification by faith. He introduces the main point in verse 21 and then provides a structured argument with supporting subpoints throughout the passage. This organised presentation allows the listeners to follow Paul's thought process and grasp the significance of justification through faith in Christ.

1. Visual and Verbal Clarity: Effective communication involves both verbal and non-verbal aspects. Verbal clarity includes enunciation, pronunciation, pacing, and vocal variety. Preachers should strive to speak clearly and audibly, ensuring the congregation's words are easily heard and understood. Variations in vocal tone, volume, and pace can also emphasise and engage the listeners.

Non-verbal communication, including body language and facial expressions, is equally important in conveying the message. A preacher's posture, gestures, and facial expressions should align with the message, enhancing its impact and authenticity. Positive and confident body language can help establish rapport with the congregation and reinforce the message's significance.

1. Audience Engagement: Engaging the congregation is vital for

effective communication. Preachers should aim to connect with the listeners emotionally and intellectually, maintaining their attention and interest throughout the sermon. This can be achieved by incorporating interactive elements, such as asking questions, encouraging responses, or inviting participation.

Jesus often engaged His audience through interactive teaching. In Matthew 16:13-16, Jesus asks His disciples, "Who do people say the Son of Man is?" and follows up with the personal question, "But what about you?... Who do you say I am?" This interaction stimulated their thinking and encouraged them to reflect on their beliefs.

The apostle Paul emphasises the importance of engaging the listeners in his letter to the Corinthians: "I came to you in weakness with great fear and trembling. My message and my preaching were not with wise and persuasive words, but with a demonstration of the Spirit's power, so that your faith might not rest on human wisdom, but on God's power" (1 Corinthians 2:3-5).

Paul's approach reminds us that effective communication is not about showcasing eloquence or human wisdom but about relying on the power of the Holy Spirit to impact hearts and minds. Engaging the congregation goes beyond mere delivery; it involves creating an environment where the Word of God can take root and transform lives.

Communicating clearly and effectively is crucial for sermon delivery. By using language that is accessible and relatable, organising the message in a logical structure, employing clear verbal and non-verbal communication, and actively engaging the congregation, preachers can enhance the effectiveness of their sermons. Ultimately, the goal is to facilitate understanding, enable the Word of God to resonate with the listeners and inspire them to respond in faith, obedience, and transformation.

Body Language and Vocal Delivery

In addition to clear and effective verbal communication, body language and vocal delivery play a significant role in sermon delivery. How preachers present themselves physically and utilise their voices can greatly enhance or detract from the message's impact. Understanding and intentionally using body language and vocal techniques can help preachers effectively engage the congregation and convey their message's passion, conviction, and sincerity.

1. Body Language: Body language refers to non-verbal cues expressed through gestures, posture, facial expressions, and movement. It is a powerful means of communication, often conveying emotions, attitudes, and intentions more effectively than words alone. Preachers can use body language to reinforce and amplify their message.

Posture: A preacher's posture can convey confidence, authority, and attentiveness. Standing upright with an open posture communicates approachability and confidence in delivering the message. It can also help establish a connection with the congregation and create an atmosphere of engagement.

Gestures: Purposeful and controlled gestures can enhance the delivery of the sermon. Gesturing can emphasise key points, illustrate concepts, and create visual interest. Jesus often used gestures to accompany His teachings, such as stretching out His hands to heal (Luke 4:40) or taking bread and wine during the Last Supper (Luke 22:19-20). These physical actions added depth and impact to His words.

Facial Expressions: The face is a powerful tool for communication. Expressive facial gestures can convey emotions, empathy, and conviction. A genuine smile, focused gaze, and appropriate facial expressions can help connect with the congregation and convey sincerity.

Movement: Purposeful movement during the sermon can create engagement and emphasise certain points. Moving closer to the congregation, walking across the stage, or using the space effectively can capture attention and maintain interest. However, excessive or distracting movements should be avoided as they can hinder the message's clarity.

1. Vocal Delivery: Vocal delivery refers to how preachers use their voices to communicate the sermon. It encompasses tone, pitch, volume, pace, and vocal variety. Effective vocal techniques can enhance the message's impact and engage the congregation emotionally.

Tone and Pitch: The tone and pitch of the preacher's voice can convey various emotions and attitudes. By adjusting the tone and pitch appropriately, preachers can express excitement, urgency, compassion, or reverence, depending on the content of the message. Matching the tone and pitch with the message's intended meaning is important.

Volume: Varying the volume of the voice can add emphasis and create dynamics in the sermon. Raising the volume during important points can capture attention and evoke a response from the congregation. Lowering the volume can create a sense of intimacy or draw the listeners in during reflective moments.

Pace: The pace at preachers speak influences the congregation's ability to process and retain information. Speaking too fast can overwhelm the listeners while speaking too slowly can lead to disengagement.

Adjusting the pace to allow for pauses, emphasising key points, or providing time for reflection can enhance comprehension and impact.

Vocal Variety: Incorporating vocal variety includes using inflexions, intonations, and variations in rhythm. This helps prevent monotony and adds depth and interest to the sermon. Just as a skilled musician plays different notes and rhythms to create a beautiful melody, a preacher can use vocal variety to engage and captivate the congregation.

The importance of body language and vocal delivery can be seen in the life and ministry of the Apostle Paul. In 1 Corinthians 2:1-5, Paul acknowledges that his preaching was not based on eloquence or persuasive words but on demonstrating the Spirit's power. However, this doesn't mean he neglected the importance of effective communication. In his letters, we can observe Paul's intentional language use and passionate delivery when addressing the churches.

For instance, in Galatians 4:12-16, Paul writes with a sense of urgency and conviction, using direct and emotive language to convey his message. He expresses his concern for the Galatian believers, employing body language and vocal delivery through his written words to communicate his earnest plea for them to return to the true gospel. Although we don't have a direct account of Paul's physical gestures or vocal tone in this context, his choice of words and the emotional weight behind them exemplify the power of effective communication.

Preachers today can learn from Paul's example and apply it to their own delivery. By being mindful of their body language—posture, gestures, facial expressions, and movement—they can amplify the message's impact and engage the congregation deeper. Similarly, by intentionally working on their vocal delivery—tone, pitch, volume, pace, and vocal variety—they can create an atmosphere that captures attention, evokes emotions, and facilitates the communication of God's Word.

Preachers need to remember that effective body language and vocal delivery are not meant to draw attention to themselves but to enhance the message and create an environment conducive to receiving and responding to the Word of God. By honing these skills, preachers can better serve the congregation by effectively conveying the truths of Scripture, inspiring transformation, and fostering a deeper connection with God.

Body language and vocal delivery are crucial components of sermon delivery. Preachers should utilise their body language effectively, employing gestures, facial expressions, posture, and movement to reinforce the message and connect with the congregation. They should also pay attention to their vocal delivery, using tone, pitch, volume, pace, and vocal variety to engage the listeners and convey the intended emotions and empathy. By honing these skills, preachers can effectively communicate the transformative power of God's Word and lead the congregation into a deeper understanding and application of biblical truths.

Engaging the Congregation

Engaging the congregation is a vital aspect of sermon delivery. It creates an atmosphere that captivates the listeners' attention, encourages active participation, and fosters a deeper connection with the communicated message. When the congregation is engaged, they are more likely to receive, internalise, and respond to the Word of God in a transformative way.

1. Interactive Elements: Incorporating interactive elements during the sermon can help engage the congregation on multiple levels. This can include asking thought-provoking questions, inviting responses or discussions, using multimedia presentations, or incorporating visual aids. Interactive elements encourage active participation and stimulate the congregation's thinking, leading to a deeper understanding and application of the message.

Jesus frequently engaged His listeners through interactive teaching methods. In Mark 8:27-29, Jesus asks His disciples, "Who do people say I am?" and follows up with the more personal question, "But what about you? Who do you say I am?" This interactive approach encouraged reflection and deepened their understanding of His identity and mission.

1. Storytelling and Illustrations: Storytelling and using illustrations can greatly enhance engagement. Jesus often used parables, relatable stories with moral or spiritual lessons, to captivate His audience and convey profound truths. Parables such as the Parable of the Good Samaritan (Luke 10:25-37) or

the Parable of the Prodigal Son (Luke 15:11-32) engaged the listeners emotionally, making the message more memorable and applicable to their lives.

Using real-life examples, personal anecdotes, or contemporary illustrations can connect biblical truths to the congregation's context and experiences. These illustrations help bridge the gap between the ancient biblical text and the present-day realities, allowing the listeners to relate to and engage with the message more deeply.

1. Application and Practical Relevance: Engaging the congregation requires demonstrating the practical relevance of the message in their daily lives. The sermon should provide theoretical knowledge and guidance on applying biblical truths to various aspects of life. Clear and actionable takeaways enable the listeners to see the direct relevance of the message and inspire them to live out their faith.

James emphasises the importance of practical application in his letter: "Do not merely listen to the word, and so deceive yourselves. Do what it says" (James 1:22). Preachers should strive to bridge the gap between hearing and doing, encouraging the congregation to apply the Word of God in their relationships, work, decision-making, and everyday interactions.

1. Authenticity and Connection: Authenticity is crucial in engaging the congregation. Preachers should convey a genuine passion for the message and a deep connection to their shared truths. When the congregation perceives the preacher's sincerity, it fosters trust. It encourages them to lean in and actively engage with the sermon.

Paul, in his letter to the Thessalonians, shares his own authenticity and connection with the believers: "Because we loved you so much, we were delighted to share with you not only the gospel of God but our lives as well" (1 Thessalonians 2:8). Paul's personal investment in their lives and his genuine love for them created a strong bond and motivated the Thessalonian believers to embrace and apply the gospel message.

Engaging the congregation is essential for effective sermon delivery. By incorporating interactive elements, storytelling, and illustrations, preachers can captivate the listeners' attention and stimulate their thinking. Demonstrating the practical relevance of the message and fostering an authentic connection with the congregation encourage active participation and application of God's Word in their lives. By intentionally engaging the congregation, preachers create an environment where the transformative power of the Word can take root and flourish.

Engaging the congregation is not merely entertaining or captivating them for the sake of it. It is about creating an environment where the truth of God's Word can be encountered and embraced. The goal is to inspire a deep connection with God and His teachings, leading to personal transformation and growth in faith.

As preachers strive to engage the congregation, they should always remember that the ultimate source of engagement and transformation is the Holy Spirit. The Spirit convicts hearts, illuminates minds and empowers individuals to respond to the message with faith and obedience. Preachers should rely on the guidance and anointing of the Holy Spirit in their sermon preparation and delivery, trusting that it is through His work that true engagement and transformation occur.

Engaging the congregation is a vital aspect of effective sermon delivery. By incorporating interactive elements, storytelling, practical application, and fostering authenticity and connection, preachers can create an environment where the congregation is captivated, challenged, and transformed by the Word of God. As they rely on the leading of the Holy Spirit, preachers can facilitate a profound encounter with God's truth, leading to lasting impact and spiritual growth in the listeners' lives.

Dealing with Nerves and Distractions

When delivering a sermon, it is common for preachers to experience nervousness or encounter distractions that can hinder their effectiveness in communicating God's Word. Preachers must address these challenges and develop strategies to overcome them, allowing the message to be delivered with clarity and impact.

1. Dependence on God's Strength: One of the first steps in dealing with nerves and distractions is recognising our dependence on God's strength. In our weakness, God's power is perfect (2 Corinthians 12:9). Preachers should approach their task humbly, acknowledging their need for the Holy Spirit's guidance, wisdom, and empowerment. Trusting in God's strength and surrendering our anxieties to Him can help alleviate nervousness and distractions, enabling preachers to focus on the task.

2. Prayer and Reflection: Prayer and reflection are powerful tools to calm our hearts and minds, especially during nervousness or distraction. Preachers can find solace and strength by praying before and during sermon preparation, seeking God's guidance, peace, and clarity. Psalm 46:10 reminds us, "Be still, and know that I am God." Taking moments of silence and reflection can help preachers centre their thoughts on God, enabling them to communicate His Word confidently and comply.

3. Preparation and Practice: Thorough preparation and practice are crucial in minimizing nervousness and distractions. Preachers should study the Scriptures, understand the message's main points, and organise their thoughts effectively.

By being well-prepared, preachers gain confidence in the content they are delivering, reducing the potential for distractions. Practising the sermon's delivery through rehearsal or recording can help preachers become more familiar and comfortable with the material, allowing them to focus on conveying the message rather than being consumed by nerves.

4. Focus on the Audience and God's Word: Redirecting focus away from self-consciousness and onto the audience and God's Word can help alleviate nervousness and distractions. Preachers should remind themselves that they are vessels chosen to deliver a message on behalf of God. Preachers can reframe their mindset and find purpose by focusing on the congregation's needs, concerns, and spiritual growth. Focusing on God's Word and its transformative power can inspire preachers to communicate with passion, conviction, and clarity, overcoming distractions and engaging the listeners effectively.

5. Embrace Vulnerability and Authenticity: Acknowledging nervousness and distractions and embracing vulnerability can enhance the connection with the congregation. Authenticity allows preachers to relate to the listeners on a human level, creating an atmosphere of empathy and understanding. In 2 Corinthians 11:30, Paul expresses his vulnerability by saying, "If I must boast, I will boast of the things that show my weakness." When preachers share their struggles and dependence on God, it can inspire the congregation to trust in God's strength rather than rely on human abilities alone.

Dealing with nerves and distractions is a common challenge for preachers. By relying on God's strength, engaging in prayer and reflection, thorough preparation and practice, focusing on the audience and God's Word, and embracing vulnerability and authenticity, preachers can effectively overcome these obstacles. Remembering that preaching is ultimately in God's hands, preachers can find confidence and peace, enabling them to communicate His Word with clarity, passion, and transformational impact.

Styles and Methods of Preaching

Preachers have various methods and styles of presenting their sermons, and the choice of approach often depends on personal preference, the context of the congregation, and the desired impact. Here are some different ways preachers can present their sermons:

1. Expository Preaching: This approach focuses on systematically and sequentially expounding the meaning of a biblical text. The preacher delves deeply into the passage, explaining its historical and cultural context, interpreting its meaning, and drawing out practical applications. Expository preaching allows the Word of God to drive the sermon, emphasising the authority and relevance of Scripture. This method is exemplified by the Apostle Paul in his epistles, where he carefully explained the truths of God's Word to the early Christian communities.

2. Topical Preaching: In this approach, the preacher selects a specific topic or theme and gathers relevant passages from different parts of the Bible to address it. The sermon explores various biblical texts and their teachings on the chosen topic, providing a comprehensive understanding. Topical preaching allows for a broader exploration of specific themes. It provides an opportunity to address relevant issues and challenges the congregation faces.

3. Narrative Preaching: This style uses storytelling techniques to convey biblical truths. The preacher selects a narrative passage, such as a parable or a story from the life of a biblical character, and unpacks its meaning and application. The goal is to engage the listeners through the power of storytelling,

drawing them into the narrative and helping them identify with the characters and situations. Jesus frequently employed this method in His teachings, using parables to convey profound spiritual truths in a relatable and memorable way.

4. Biographical Preaching: This approach centres around the life and experiences of a specific biblical character. The preacher explores the character's stories, highlighting their strengths, weaknesses, victories, and challenges, and draws lessons and principles that apply to the listeners' lives. By examining the lives of individuals like David, Moses, or Peter, the preacher provides practical insights into faith, obedience, perseverance, and other aspects of the Christian journey.

5. Persuasive Preaching: This style aims to appeal to the emotions, intellect, and will of the listeners, with an emphasis on motivating them to respond and make a decision. The preacher utilises rhetorical techniques, compelling arguments, and passionate delivery to persuade the congregation to embrace a particular belief or course of action. This method can be seen in the sermons of the Apostle Peter, particularly in Acts 2, where he passionately calls the crowd to repentance and faith in Jesus Christ.

6. Interactive Preaching: This style involves engaging the congregation in a participatory manner. The preacher may include opportunities for dialogue, questions and answers, small group discussions, or other interactive elements during the sermon. This approach fosters active engagement, encourages personal reflection, and enhances the congregation's understanding and application of the message.

It's important to note that while different preaching styles exist, the ultimate goal is to faithfully communicate God's Word, inspire transformation, and glorify Him. The chosen approach should align with the preacher's strengths, the congregation's needs, and the Holy Spirit's leading. Regardless of the specific style, effective preaching is marked by clarity, relevance, authenticity, and a reliance on the power of the Holy Spirit to impact the hearts and lives of the listeners.

Practical Tips for Sermon Delivery

———

Practical tips for sermon delivery:

1. Prepare and Practice: Adequate preparation is essential for effective sermon delivery. Study the passage, organise your thoughts, and create a clear outline. Practice your sermon multiple times to become familiar with the content, flow, and timing. As Paul encouraged Timothy in 2 Timothy 2:15, "Do your best to present yourself to God as one approved, a worker who does not need to be ashamed and who correctly handles the word of truth."

2. Communicate with Clarity: Use clear and concise language to communicate your message. Avoid jargon or overly complex terms that may confuse the listeners. Strive for simplicity and ensure your main points and applications are easily understood. Paul emphasises the importance of clarity in 1 Corinthians 14:9, "So it is with you. Unless you speak intelligible words with your tongue, how will anyone know what you are saying? You will just be speaking into the air."

3. Engage the Congregation: Establish eye contact with the congregation and maintain good posture and body language. Vary your tone, volume, and pace to keep the listeners engaged. Use gestures and facial expressions to emphasise key points. Jesus, in His teachings, often engaged the crowds through His compelling presence and manner of speaking.

4. Connect Emotionally: Connect with the emotions of your listeners by using appropriate illustrations, stories, and examples. Appeal to their hearts and minds, as emotions can enhance the impact and memorability of your message. Jesus

often connected with people on an emotional level, such as when He showed compassion for the crowds or expressed righteous anger at religious hypocrisy.

5. Utilise Visual Aids: Incorporate visual aids, such as slides or props, to enhance understanding and retention. Visual elements can help reinforce key points, visually represent concepts, and engage visual learners in the congregation. Using visuals is not meant to overshadow the message but to supplement and reinforce it.

6. Allow for Silence and Pause: Embrace moments of silence and intentional pauses during your sermon. It gives the listeners time to reflect on what has been shared and allows the Holy Spirit to work in their hearts. Silence can create a sense of anticipation and highlight the weight of the message. As Ecclesiastes 3:7 reminds us, there is "a time to be silent and a time to speak."

7. Respond to the Holy Spirit's Leading: Remain sensitive to the leading of the Holy Spirit during your sermon delivery. Be open to promptings or deviations from your prepared notes if you sense the Spirit directing you to address specific needs or concerns in the congregation. Allow the Spirit to guide your words and bring forth the timely message that God desires to communicate.

8. Seek Feedback and Evaluation: Request feedback from trusted individuals who can provide constructive criticism and insights to help improve your sermon delivery. Evaluate your own sermons and identify areas of strength and areas that need improvement. Continual growth and refinement in sermon delivery are essential for effective ministry.

Remember, effective sermon delivery is not about performance but about faithfully communicating God's Word in a way that engages and impacts the congregation. As Paul encourages in Colossians 4:6, "Let your conversation be always full of grace, seasoned with salt, so that you may know how to answer everyone." May your sermon delivery be marked by grace, clarity, and the power of the Holy Spirit.

Sermon Notes: Practical Tips

Sermon notes. Some practical tips for preachers:

1. Familiarise Yourself with the Notes: Before stepping onto the pulpit, familiarise yourself with your sermon notes. Review the structure, main points, and supporting scriptures. Understand the message flow so you can navigate through your notes smoothly.

2. Use Clear and Concise Notes: Ensure your sermon notes are concisely organised. Use bullet points, headings, and subheadings to make it easy to follow. Avoid overcrowding your notes with excessive information or cluttered formatting that may confuse you during delivery.

3. Highlight Key Phrases or Keywords: Consider using highlighters or underlining key phrases or keywords in your notes. This can help you quickly identify and emphasise important points without reading every word verbatim. Highlighting also serves as a visual cue to draw your attention to essential elements of your sermon.

4. Practice Transitions: Work on seamless transitions between different sections or points in your sermon. This will help you maintain a natural flow and avoid interruptions or awkward pauses while referring to your notes. Practice moving from one point to another without losing momentum or losing the engagement of your listeners.

5. Use Visual Prompts or Symbols: Incorporate visual prompts or symbols within your notes to help you remember certain cues or actions during delivery. For example, you can use arrows to remind yourself to make eye contact with the

congregation, use a smiley face as a reminder to bring warmth and enthusiasm to a particular section or draw a small cross as a reminder to emphasise a specific biblical truth.

6. Practice Eye Contact: When referring to your notes when needed, making intentional eye contact with the congregation is important. Establishing eye contact helps you connect with your listeners and conveys authenticity and engagement. Glancing at your notes and then looking up to maintain eye contact creates a balance between referencing your notes and connecting with the congregation.

7. Utilise Mnemonic Devices: Consider using mnemonic devices or memory aids to help you recall key points or scriptures. These can be acronyms, memorable phrases, or word associations that trigger your memory. For example, you can create a memorable acronym for the main points of your sermon or use alliteration to remember a series of supporting verses.

8. Develop Confidence in Your Preparation: Build confidence in your sermon through thorough study and practice. The more familiar you are with the content, the less you need to rely heavily on your notes. Spend ample time internalising the message so that referring to your notes becomes a tool to support your delivery rather than a crutch.

9. Stay Flexible and Responsive: While having sermon notes is important, remain open to the leading of the Holy Spirit during your sermon. Be willing to deviate from your notes if the Spirit prompts you to address specific needs or opportunities for spontaneous insights or illustrations. Trust in God's guidance as you rely on both your prepared notes and the promptings of the Spirit.

10. Seek Feedback and Make Improvements: After each sermon, take time to evaluate your use of sermon notes. Seek feedback

from trusted individuals who can provide constructive criticism and insights on how you can improve. Learn from each preaching experience and make necessary adjustments to enhance your ability to refer to your notes effectively.

Remember, sermon notes are meant to be a helpful tool, not a hindrance. The goal is to rely on them for support while maintaining a genuine and engaging connection with the congregation. By implementing these practical tips, you can confidently refer to your sermon notes and deliver a powerful and impactful message to those listening.

The Preacher's Sermon Notes

———

When preparing a sermon, preachers have different approaches to organising their material. Two common methods are writing a full sermon and using an outline. Each method has its advantages and disadvantages, and there are other options. Let's explore them in detail:

1. Writing Out a Sermon in Full:

Advantages:

- Clarity and Precision: Writing out a sermon in full allows you to articulate your thoughts precisely. It helps ensure that your message is clear and organised.
- Thorough Preparation: Writing out a sermon forces you to delve deeply into the text, study it carefully, and develop a well-structured message.
- Confidence in Delivery: A fully written sermon gives you a sense of security and confidence in delivering the message. You have all the content and can follow it verbatim if desired.

Disadvantages:

- Dependency on Manuscript: Relying heavily on a written script can hinder eye contact and engagement with the congregation. It may restrict spontaneity and flexibility in responding to the leading of the Holy Spirit.
- Risk of Monotony: Reading from a manuscript can sometimes lead to a monotonous delivery, as it may lack the natural flow and enthusiasm from speaking more extemporaneously.
- Time and Effort: Writing out a sermon in full requires

significant time and effort, which may not be feasible for preachers with busy schedules.

1. Using an Outline:

Advantages:

- Flexibility and Adaptability: An outline provides a flexible framework to guide your sermon. It allows room for improvisation, adaptability, and responsiveness to the congregation's needs or the leading of the Holy Spirit.
- Enhanced Engagement: With an outline, you can maintain better eye contact with the congregation, fostering a stronger connection. It allows for a more conversational and interactive delivery style.
- Efficient Preparation: Creating an outline is generally less time-consuming than writing out a sermon in full. It allows you to focus on the main points and structure of the message.

Disadvantages:

- Potential Lack of Clarity: Depending on the level of detail in the outline, there is a risk of insufficient clarity or coherence in communicating complex ideas or supporting arguments.
- Need for Preparation: While an outline provides flexibility, it requires thorough preparation to ensure the content is well-developed and coherent. Without proper preparation, relying solely on an outline may lead to a disorganised or incomplete sermon.

1. Other Options:
    - Hybrid Approach: Some preachers adopt a hybrid approach, combining elements of writing out a

sermon and using an outline. They may write out the introduction and conclusion verbatim while using an outline for the main body of the sermon. This approach maintains clarity for crucial sections while allowing flexibility in delivery.

- ◦ Manuscript with Markings: Another option is using a manuscript with strategic markings, such as highlighting key phrases, underlining important points, or using symbols to trigger specific actions or illustrations during delivery. This approach allows for a balance between having a written script and maintaining engagement with the congregation.

Ultimately, the choice between writing out a sermon in full, using an outline, or adopting a hybrid approach depends on personal preference, preaching style, and the specific needs of each sermon. It's important to experiment and find the method that best suits your preparation style and enables effective delivery while maintaining connection and engagement with the congregation. Prayerful consideration, feedback from trusted individuals, and regular reflection on sermon delivery can help you refine your approach and continually improve as a preacher.

6. Evaluating the Sermon

Evaluating the sermon is a vital aspect of the preaching process. It involves reflecting on the effectiveness of the message and delivery, seeking feedback from others, and making necessary improvements and adjustments. Through thoughtful evaluation, preachers can grow their skills, refine their message, and better serve the congregation.

Point 6 delves into the importance of personal reflection, seeking feedback, and the ongoing process of improving and adjusting the sermon. It recognises that no sermon is perfect, and there is always room for growth and refinement in the preacher's craft.

The evaluation process allows preachers to assess their effectiveness in communicating God's Word and engaging the congregation. It helps identify strengths to build upon and areas for improvement. By critically analysing their sermons, preachers can enhance their delivery, clarify their message, and ensure a greater impact on the listeners' lives.

Seeking feedback from others is an invaluable part of the evaluation process. Constructive feedback from trusted mentors, fellow preachers, or congregation members provides valuable insights and perspectives. It helps preachers better understand how others receive and interpret their message, enabling them to refine their approach and address any potential weaknesses.

The effective evaluation also involves ongoing self-development. Preachers should be committed to continuous learning, seeking to expand their knowledge of Scripture, improve their communication skills, and stay abreast of cultural and societal trends. Prepreachers can stay relevant and impactful in their preaching ministry by engaging with various resources, attending seminars or conferences, and seeking growth opportunities.

The evaluation of the sermon plays a crucial role in the preacher's growth and the effectiveness of their message. Through personal reflection, seeking feedback, and ongoing self-development, preachers can refine their skills, improve their delivery, and better serve the congregation. The evaluation process is not one of self-criticism but rather a commitment to excellence and a desire to continually grow in the proclamation of God's Word. By embracing evaluation as an integral part of the preaching journey, preachers can become more effective communicators, ultimately transforming lives and advancing God's kingdom.

Personal Reflection and Evaluation

Personal reflection and evaluation are essential to sermon preparation and delivery. It involves the preacher taking time to assess their performance, discern their message's effectiveness, and identify areas for growth and improvement. Through personal reflection, preachers can deepen their understanding of their strengths and weaknesses, refine their preaching style, and cultivate a greater sense of authenticity and effectiveness in their ministry.

Personal reflection begins with a humble and honest examination of the preacher's heart and motives. It is essential to ensure that the preacher's motivations align with God's purposes and that they are faithfully seeking to communicate His truth rather than seeking personal recognition or validation. This introspective process requires preachers to examine their intentions, attitudes, and sincerity in proclaiming the Word of God.

In addition to self-reflection, evaluating the content of the sermon is crucial. Preachers should assess the clarity and coherence of their message, ensuring that it aligns with the teachings of Scripture and effectively communicates the intended biblical truths. It involves examining the sermon's structure, flow, and organisation and assessing if the main points and supporting arguments are clear and logical.

Scripture emphasises the importance of self-examination and personal reflection. In Psalm 139:23-24, David prays, "Search me, O God, and know my heart! Try me and know my thoughts! And see if there be any grievous way in me, and lead me in the way everlasting." This prayer demonstrates David's desire for God to examine his inner being and reveal any areas that need correction.

Similarly, Paul exhorts Timothy in 1 Timothy 4:16 to "keep a close watch on yourself and the teaching. Persist in this, for you will save yourself and your hearers." This verse highlights the importance of self-examination and diligence in ensuring the accuracy and impact of the message.

Personal reflection also involves considering the preacher's delivery and communication skills. Preachers should assess their vocal tone, body language, and overall engagement with the congregation. Evaluating whether the delivery effectively conveys the intended emotions and engages the listeners meaningfully is important. Preachers should consider their use of illustrations, application of biblical truths to everyday life, and the overall impact their delivery has on the congregation.

Through personal reflection and evaluation, preachers can identify areas for improvement and make necessary adjustments to their preaching. This ongoing process fosters growth, deepens spiritual maturity, and enhances the preacher's ability to effectively communicate God's Word.

Personal reflection and evaluation are integral to the preaching process. By honestly assessing one's heart, examining the content and structure of the sermon, and evaluating the delivery and impact, preachers can cultivate authenticity, deepen their understanding of their strengths and weaknesses, and continually strive for excellence in communicating God's Word. Through self-reflection, preachers can align their motives with God's purposes, ensure biblical accuracy, and engage the congregation with clarity and relevance. Personal reflection and evaluation ultimately lead to growth, transformation, and a more impactful preaching ministry.

Feedback from Others

Seeking feedback from others is valuable in evaluating the sermon and improving one's preaching skills. Feedback provides an external perspective, offering insights, observations, and constructive criticism that can enhance the preacher's effectiveness in communicating God's Word. By humbly receiving and discerning feedback, preachers can better understand how their message is received and make necessary adjustments to better serve the congregation.

There are various sources from which preachers can seek feedback:

1. Mentors and Fellow Preachers: Trusted mentors and experienced fellow preachers can provide invaluable guidance and feedback. They can offer insights based on their preaching experiences, providing constructive criticism and suggesting areas for improvement. Proverbs 27:17 states, "As iron sharpens iron, so one person sharpens another." Seeking feedback from mentors and peers allows preachers to sharpen their skills, refine their message, and grow in their calling.

2. Congregation Members: Feedback from the congregation is also essential as it represents the listeners' perspective. Congregation members can provide insights into how the sermon impacted their lives, what resonated with them, and areas where they may have felt disconnected. Their feedback can help preachers understand the congregation's needs, concerns, and questions, allowing for more relevant and impactful preaching. However, it is important to note that feedback from the congregation should be approached with discernment, considering both the individual's perspective

and the overall consensus.

3. Evaluation Forms or Surveys: Implementing evaluation forms or surveys can effectively gather feedback from the congregation anonymously. These forms can include questions about the message's clarity, the content's relevance, and the sermon's impact on their spiritual growth. By collecting anonymous feedback, preachers can receive honest responses, providing valuable insights to guide their improvement efforts.

When receiving feedback, preachers need to approach it with humility and a willingness to learn and grow. Proverbs 12:15 reminds us, "The way of fools seems right to them, but the wise listen to advice." Embracing a teachable spirit allows preachers to discern the constructive elements in the feedback and make necessary adjustments without becoming defensive or discouraged.

While feedback is valuable, preachers should also exercise discernment in assessing and applying it. Not all feedback may be relevant or beneficial, and it is important to filter it through the lens of Scripture and personal conviction. Preachers should prayerfully consider the feedback received, seeking the guidance of the Holy Spirit to discern what aligns with God's Word and what can contribute to their growth as effective gospel communicators.

Seeking feedback from others is an important aspect of sermon evaluation and growth as a preacher. By humbly receiving feedback from mentors, fellow preachers, and congregation members, preachers can gain valuable insights, perspectives, and suggestions for improvement. Proverbs 11:14 says, "Where there is no guidance, a people falls, but in an abundance of counsellors, there is safety." Engaging in a dialogue with others about the sermon helps preachers refine their message, address blind spots and deepen their impact on the lives of their listeners.

However, it is crucial to approach feedback with discernment, filtering it through the lens of Scripture and personal conviction. Not all feedback may be applicable or align with the preacher's unique calling and style. Ultimately, the preacher's primary focus should be on faithfully proclaiming God's Word and shepherding the congregation entrusted to their care.

By combining personal reflection and feedback from others, preachers can embark on a journey of growth, continually improving their preaching skills and deepening their impact on the lives of their listeners. Through a humble and teachable spirit, preachers can create an environment that fosters growth for themselves and their congregation. By seeking feedback, preachers demonstrate their commitment to excellence, love for the congregation, and desire to effectively communicate the life-transforming message of the gospel.

Making Improvements and Adjustments

This section focuses on improving and adjusting the sermon based on personal reflection and feedback. It recognises that no sermon is perfect and that there is always room for growth and refinement in the preacher's delivery and message. By actively seeking to improve and adjust, preachers can enhance their effectiveness in communicating God's Word and engage the congregation more effectively.

Making improvements and adjustments begins with carefully reviewing the personal reflection and feedback received. Preachers should prayerfully consider the insights and observations provided, discerning what aligns with God's Word and what can enhance their preaching ministry. It requires a humble and teachable spirit, willing to acknowledge areas for improvement and actively seek ways to address them.

One aspect of making improvements is refining the content of the sermon. This involves evaluating the message's clarity, relevance, and biblical accuracy. Preachers should ensure that their sermons align with the teachings of Scripture and effectively convey the intended biblical truths. Paul exhorted Timothy in 2 Timothy 2:15, saying, "Do your best to present yourself to God as one approved, a worker who has no need to be ashamed, rightly handling the word of truth." This verse emphasises the importance of faithfully handling God's Word, which requires continuous study, reflection, and refinement.

Preachers should consider the structure and organisation of their sermons. This includes evaluating the coherence and logical flow of the message. Are the main points clear and well-supported? Is there a progression that leads to a meaningful conclusion? By analysing the sermon's structure, preachers can ensure that their message is delivered in a way that is engaging, easy to follow, and conducive to effective communication.

The feedback received from mentors, fellow preachers, and congregation members can provide specific areas for improvement. It may include suggestions for enhancing delivery, incorporating more relevant illustrations, or deepening application to everyday life. Preachers should prayerfully consider this feedback and discern how to implement it in a way that aligns with their preaching style and the needs of their specific congregation.

The process of making improvements and adjustments is ongoing. It requires preachers to continually seek growth and development in their preaching ministry. This includes studying God's Word, staying informed about current events and cultural trends, and exploring different preaching techniques and approaches. By being intentional about self-improvement, preachers can become more effective communicators, capable of engaging the congregation meaningfully.

Making improvements and adjustments to the sermon is integral to the preacher's growth and effectiveness. By carefully evaluating personal reflection and feedback, preachers can refine their sermons' content, structure, and delivery. Through continuous study, prayerful discernment, and a commitment to personal growth, preachers can enhance their ability to communicate God's Word and impact the lives of their listeners. As Paul urged the Corinthian believers in 1 Corinthians 14:12, "Since you are eager for manifestations of the Spirit, strive to excel in building up the church." This verse reminds us of the importance of striving for excellence in preaching, seeking to build up and edify the body of Christ through the proclamation of the gospel.

7. Preaching in Various Contexts

Preaching is a dynamic and transformative ministry not limited to a single context. Throughout history, preachers have been called to proclaim the Word of God in diverse settings, addressing different age groups, non-Christian audiences, and varying cultural contexts. This chapter explores the challenges and opportunities of preaching in various contexts, emphasising the importance of adapting the message without compromising the core truths of the gospel.

In a world marked by cultural diversity, technological advancements, and evolving societal norms, preachers must navigate the complexities of different contexts to effectively communicate the timeless message of God's Word. Whether preaching to children, teenagers, adults, non-Christians, or in cross-cultural settings, preachers are tasked with presenting the gospel in a relevant, engaging, and transformative way.

We will highlight the need for preachers to understand different contexts' unique characteristics, needs, and challenges. It explores practical strategies for tailoring the message to connect with specific audiences while remaining faithful to biblical teachings. Preaching in various contexts requires sensitivity, cultural intelligence, and a deep reliance on the Holy Spirit's guidance.

By delving into the nuances of preaching in different age groups, non-Christian audiences, and diverse cultural settings, preachers can equip themselves with the tools to effectively engage listeners and bring about spiritual transformation. Each context presents opportunities and challenges, demanding a thoughtful and intentional approach to proclaiming the gospel.

Ultimately, preaching in various contexts aims to bridge the gap between the eternal truth of God's Word and the specific needs and experiences of the listeners. By contextualising the message while preserving its core principles, preachers can effectively communicate the unchanging truth of the gospel in ways that resonate with different audiences and cultures.

This chapter will delve into the practical considerations, biblical principles, and effective strategies for preaching in different contexts. It will explore how preachers can adapt their preaching style, language, illustrations, and application to effectively reach various age groups, engage non-Christian audiences, and minister in different cultural settings. This section aims to empower preachers to effectively proclaim the gospel message, break down barriers, and impact diverse audiences by equipping preachers with insights and guidance.

Preaching in various contexts is an essential aspect of the preacher's ministry. It requires a deep understanding of different audiences and cultures' unique characteristics, needs, and challenges. By adapting the message without compromising the core truths of the gospel, preachers can effectively engage listeners, bridge cultural gaps, and transform the lives of those they serve. This chapter will provide valuable insights and practical guidance to equip preachers for the dynamic and transformative task of preaching in diverse contexts.

Preaching Different Age Groups

Preaching different age groups requires a tailored approach, recognising each group's distinct developmental stages, interests, and needs. Effective communication of God's Word to children, teenagers, and adults involves adapting the message, language, illustrations, and application to engage and edify each age group.

When preaching to children, it is essential to convey biblical truths in a way that is understandable and relatable to their level of comprehension. Jesus Himself emphasised the importance of ministering to children, saying in Matthew 19:14, "Let the little children come to me and do not hinder them, for to such belongs the kingdom of heaven." Preachers should aim to present the gospel in a manner that captures the imagination and attention of children, utilising simple language, vibrant illustrations, and interactive elements. Incorporating stories, parables, and practical examples can help children grasp biblical concepts and apply them to their daily lives.

Teenagers face unique challenges and are in a critical stage of identity formation. Preaching to teenagers requires addressing their questions, doubts, and struggles while providing them with a solid biblical foundation. Paul's encouragement to Timothy in 1 Timothy 4:12 is relevant in this context: "Let no one despise you for your youth, but set the believers an example in speech, in conduct, in love, in faith, in purity." Preachers should strive to connect with teenagers through relevant topics, contemporary examples, and authentic engagement. Applying biblical principles to their real-life situations and challenges can help them navigate their faith journey and develop a deeper relationship with God.

When preaching to adults, preachers encounter diverse life experiences, spiritual maturity levels, and intellectual capacities. The apostle Paul recognised the need to adapt his message to different audiences, stating in 1 Corinthians 9:22-23, "I have become all things to all people, that by all means, I might save some. I do it all for the gospel's sake, which I may share with them in its blessings." Preachers should employ a balanced approach, using clear biblical exposition, practical application, and thoughtful illustrations that resonate with adults' life experiences and challenges. Engaging the mind and the heart is crucial in inspiring spiritual growth and transformation.

Adapting the message to different age groups does not mean compromising the core truths of the gospel. The fundamental biblical teachings remain unchanged, but the message's delivery and contextualisation vary. Hebrews 5:12-13 highlights the importance of growth and maturity in understanding God's Word: "For though by this time you ought to be teachers, you need someone to teach you again the basic principles of the oracles of God. You need milk, not solid food." Preachers should aim to facilitate spiritual growth, moving listeners from foundational truths to deeper theological concepts as they mature in their faith.

Involving parents and caregivers in the spiritual nurture of children and teenagers is crucial. Preachers can support and equip parents with biblical principles and practical guidance, recognising that the family plays a significant role in shaping the faith of younger generations. Deuteronomy 6:6-7 instructs parents, saying, "And these words that I command you today shall be on your heart. You shall teach them diligently to your children and shall talk of them when you sit in your house, and when you walk by the way, and when you lie down, and when you rise."

Preaching different age groups requires a thoughtful and intentional approach. By adapting the message, language, illustrations, and application, preachers can effectively engage and minister to children, teenagers, and adults. By recognising the developmental stages, needs, and challenges of each age group, preachers can present the timeless truths of God in ways that resonate with their specific contexts. The goal is to facilitate understanding, foster spiritual growth, and inspire a deeper relationship with God.

Preaching to different age groups is a privilege and a responsibility. It allows preachers to sow seeds of faith, nurture young hearts and minds, and guide individuals through various stages of spiritual development. By applying biblical principles and utilising age-appropriate methods, preachers can create environments where children, teenagers, and adults can encounter God's truth, experience His love, and grow in their faith.

In the next sections of this point, we will explore practical strategies, biblical insights, and effective approaches for preaching to different age groups. We will delve into each age group's unique characteristics, needs, and challenges, considering how to effectively communicate the gospel message in engaging, relevant, and transformative ways. By carefully understanding the target audience, preachers can ensure that the Word of God impacts the lives of children, teenagers, and adults, leading them to a deeper understanding of God's love and truth.

Preaching to different age groups is essential to the preacher's ministry. It involves adapting the message, language, illustrations, and application to effectively engage and minister to children, teenagers, and adults. By recognising each age group's developmental stages, needs, and challenges, preachers can present the timeless truths of God's Word in ways that resonate with their specific contexts. By faithfully proclaiming the gospel and facilitating spiritual growth, preachers can impact the lives of individuals across generations, guiding them toward a vibrant and transformative relationship with God.

Preaching Non-Christian Audiences

Preaching to non-Christian audiences presents a unique set of challenges and opportunities. It requires a thoughtful and intentional approach to effectively communicate the gospel to those unfamiliar with biblical concepts or Christian beliefs. Preachers engaging with non-Christians have the important task of presenting the truth of the gospel in a way that is compelling, relevant, and accessible.

The apostle Paul serves as an excellent example of reaching non-Christian audiences. In Acts 17, Paul preached to the philosophers and intellectuals in Athens. He observed their religious practices and engaged with their worldview before proclaiming the truth of the gospel in a manner that resonated with their culture and beliefs. Paul's approach demonstrates the importance of contextualisation and understanding the audience when preaching to non-Christians.

When preaching to non-Christian audiences, preachers should seek to build bridges of understanding, addressing their questions, doubts, and objections. The goal is to communicate the love of God, the redemptive work of Christ, and the gospel's relevance to their lives. Paul emphasised the importance of contextualisation in 1 Corinthians 9:22, stating, "I have become all things to all people, that by all means, I might save some." This approach requires sensitivity to the audience's cultural, intellectual, and spiritual context, allowing the message to resonate with their needs and concerns.

Effective communication with non-Christians often involves using relatable language, analogies, and illustrations that connect with their experiences and frames of reference. Jesus often employed parables, stories, and real-life examples to convey deep spiritual truths that engaged His listeners. By using similar approaches, preachers can communicate the gospel message in ways that are accessible and meaningful to non-Christian audiences.

Engaging in genuine dialogue and actively listening to the questions, objections, and concerns of non-Christians is also crucial. Peter encouraged believers in 1 Peter 3:15 to "always be prepared to make a defence to anyone who asks you for a reason for the hope in you." This requires a deep understanding of the gospel and a willingness to engage in respectful and compassionate conversations that address the specific needs and challenges of non-Christians.

Preachers should rely on the power of the Holy Spirit when preaching to non-Christian audiences. The apostle Paul recognised that the Holy Spirit convicts and brings about spiritual transformation. In 1 Corinthians 2:4, he says, "My message and my preaching were not with wise and persuasive words but with a demonstration of the Spirit's power." Preachers must depend on the work of the Holy Spirit to open hearts and minds to the gospel's truth.

Preaching to non-Christian audiences requires a thoughtful and intentional approach. By understanding the audience's cultural, intellectual, and spiritual context, preachers can effectively communicate the gospel message in ways that resonate with their needs and concerns. Through contextualisation, relatable language, genuine dialogue, and reliance on the Holy Spirit, preachers can engage non-Christians and guide them towards a personal encounter with Jesus Christ. By faithfully proclaiming the truth and demonstrating the gospel's transformative power, preachers play a vital role in leading non-Christians to salvation and a vibrant relationship with God.

Preaching in Different Cultural Settings

Preaching in different cultural settings requires awareness and sensitivity to the specific culture's unique customs, traditions, and values. It involves understanding how culture influences worldview, communication styles, and the reception of the gospel message. Effective cross-cultural preaching aims to bridge the gap between the timeless truths of Scripture and the cultural context in which it is proclaimed.

The Bible provides examples of how the gospel was communicated in various cultural settings. In Acts 17, when Paul preached in Athens, he engaged with the philosophical and religious beliefs of the Greeks, even referencing their altar to the "unknown god" (Acts 17:23). Paul recognised the cultural context and used it as a starting point to present the truth of the gospel to the Athenians. This demonstrates the importance of cultural sensitivity and contextualisation when preaching in different cultural settings.

Preachers should be aware of cultural nuances, values, and practices that may impact the reception of the gospel message. They should seek to understand the worldview, religious beliefs, and social dynamics of the culture they minister. By doing so, they can effectively communicate biblical truths in a relevant and relatable way to the cultural context.

At the same time, preachers must remain faithful to the unchanging truths of Scripture. The gospel message should never be compromised or diluted to accommodate cultural preferences. The apostle Paul emphasised the importance of preserving the integrity of the gospel message in Galatians 1:8-9, declaring, "But even if we or an angel from heaven should preach to you a gospel contrary to the one we preached to you, let him be accursed." Preachers must ensure that they communicate the central message of salvation through faith in Jesus Christ, even as they navigate the cultural nuances.

An effective approach to preaching in different cultural settings involves identifying points of connection and common ground with the culture. This can be done by using culturally relevant examples, illustrations, and stories that resonate with the experiences and values of the audience. Jesus Himself often used parables and stories familiar to His listeners, drawing from their everyday lives to convey spiritual truths.

Preachers should strive to promote cultural sensitivity and unity within the body of Christ. The diversity of cultures within the church should be celebrated and embraced, recognising that all believers are united in Christ. The apostle Paul addressed the importance of unity in Ephesians 4:4-6, stating, "There is one body and one Spirit—just as you were called to the one hope that belongs to your call—one Lord, one faith, one baptism, one God and Father of all, who is over all and through all and in all." Preachers can foster an environment where different cultural perspectives are valued and contribute to the richness of the church community.

Preaching in different cultural settings requires understanding the cultural context, sensitivity to cultural nuances, and a commitment to faithfully communicate the gospel message. By recognising the influence of culture on worldview and communication styles, preachers can effectively bridge the gap between the timeless truths of Scripture and the cultural context in which they minister. Cultural sensitivity, contextualisation, and the promotion of unity within the body of Christ are essential in engaging diverse cultural settings with the gospel's transformative power. Preachers have the privilege of proclaiming the unchanging truth of God's Word in ways that resonate with the hearts and minds of people from various cultures, leading them to a deeper understanding of God's love and truth.

8. The Role of Preaching in the Life of the Church

This chapter explores the significant role of preaching in the church's life. Preaching is not simply a task or an obligation but a vital component of worship, discipleship, and evangelism. It serves as a means through which God's Word is proclaimed, hearts are transformed, and the church's mission is advanced. Understanding the multifaceted role of preaching helps us appreciate its importance and impact within the context of the church community.

This section will delve into the various dimensions of preaching and its significance in the church's life. We will examine how preaching is an act of worship, offering a space where the congregation can encounter God and respond to His truth. We will explore how preaching functions as a discipleship tool, nurturing and equipping believers for spiritual growth and maturity. We will discuss how preaching serves as a means of evangelism, reaching out to non-believers and inviting them to experience the gospel's transformative power.

The role of preaching in the church's life goes beyond a mere informative or educational function. It is a dynamic and transformative encounter with God's Word, facilitated by the preacher's faithful exposition and application of Scripture. Preaching is an act of faithfulness to God's calling, a stewardship of the message entrusted to preachers, and a response to the great commission to make disciples of all nations (Matthew 28:19-20).

As we explore the multifaceted role of preaching in the church's life, we will discover how it intertwines with other aspects of Christian worship, discipleship, and evangelism. We will explore the biblical foundations and theological underpinnings that highlight the centrality of preaching in the early church and its continued significance in contemporary times.

This chapter will provide a comprehensive understanding of the role of preaching in the life of the church. It is not merely a task or a formality but a sacred privilege and responsibility. Preaching leads the church in worship, fosters discipleship, and proclaims the good news of salvation to a world in need. By recognising the significance of preaching and embracing its transformative power, the church can grow in its devotion to God, deepen its understanding of His Word, and fulfil its mission to make disciples of all nations.

Preaching as Worship

Preaching holds a central place in the worship of the church. It is an act of worship and facilitates the congregation's engagement with God's Word, leading them into a deeper encounter with Him. Preaching as worship involves honouring God, exalting Christ, and inviting the Holy Spirit's presence and work among the worshipping community.

The foundation of preaching as worship can be traced back to the biblical precedent of the public reading and teaching of Scripture in the Old Testament. In Nehemiah 8, we see Ezra, the scribe, bringing the book of the Law before the assembly of people. He read the Law aloud and explained its meaning, and the people responded with worship and obedience. The act of proclaiming God's Word ignited a collective response of praise and adoration, demonstrating the transformative power of the Scriptures.

In the New Testament, the early church continued gathering to devote themselves to the apostles' teaching (Acts 2:42). The apostles were entrusted with proclaiming the gospel message, teaching the believers, and equipping them for ministry. The preaching of the Word was an integral part of their worship gatherings, strengthening the faith of believers and fostering spiritual growth.

When the Word of God is faithfully proclaimed, it becomes a catalyst for worship. The preacher stands as a conduit through which God's truth is conveyed, drawing the attention and affection of the congregation towards the Lord. Preaching becomes an offering of praise and thanksgiving as the preacher, under the guidance of the Holy

Spirit, expounds upon God's majesty, grace, and mercy revealed in His Word.

Preaching as worship involves the congregation's response to God's Word. As the Word is proclaimed, it calls for a response of faith, repentance, and surrender. The listeners are invited to engage with the Scriptures, allowing them to penetrate their hearts and transform their lives. James 1:22 encourages believers to be doers of the Word, not merely hearers. Preaching as worship inspires the congregation to respond in obedience, devotion, and adoration, deepening their relationship with God.

The content and focus of preaching contribute to the worship experience. Preaching that exalts Christ, lifts His name high, and magnifies His redemptive work on the cross enables the congregation to enter a place of adoration and awe. The proclamation of the gospel message, the declaration of God's attributes, and the exploration of His Word all lead the worshipping community to respond with praise and worship.

Preaching as worship acknowledges the profound impact of the Word of God on the worship experience of the church. As the Scriptures are faithfully proclaimed, the congregation is led into a deeper encounter with God, responding in awe, adoration, and obedience. Preaching becomes a vital component of worship, honouring God, exalting Christ, and inviting the transformative work of the Holy Spirit. By recognising the role of preaching as an act of worship, the church can engage in worship services centred on God's Word, filled with reverence, and conducive to spiritual growth and transformation.

Preaching as Discipleship

Preaching plays a crucial role in discipleship within the church. It serves as a means through which believers are nurtured, equipped, and encouraged to grow in their faith and become mature followers of Christ. Preaching as discipleship involves intentionally and systematically teaching God's Word to develop spiritual maturity and foster a deepening relationship with Christ.

The foundation for preaching as discipleship can be found in Jesus' commission to His disciples in Matthew 28:19-20, commonly known as the Great Commission. Jesus instructs His followers to make disciples of all nations, baptising and teaching them to observe all He commanded. The teaching aspect of disciple-making aligns with the role of preaching in the church. Through preaching, believers are instructed in the truths of Scripture, guided in applying biblical principles, and encouraged in their walk with Christ.

In his letters to various churches, the apostle Paul demonstrates the importance of preaching as discipleship. In Ephesians 4:11-13, Paul speaks about the various ministry roles within the church, including pastors and teachers. He explains that these individuals are given to equip the saints for the work of ministry and for building up the body of Christ until we all attain the unity of the faith and the knowledge of the Son of God. Preaching serves as a tool for equipping believers, helping them grow in their understanding of the faith and their knowledge of Christ.

Preaching as discipleship involves the systematic teaching and exposition of Scripture. It aims to give believers a comprehensive understanding of God's Word, enabling them to apply its principles daily. Through preaching, believers are guided in biblical doctrine, taught moral and ethical principles, and encouraged to live out their faith practically. Preaching also addresses relevant issues and challenges believers may face, providing guidance and wisdom from God's Word.

Preaching as discipleship fosters spiritual transformation and maturity. It challenges believers to grow in their faith, deepen their relationship with Christ, and conform to His likeness. The apostle Paul expresses his desire for the spiritual growth and maturity of the believers in Colossians 1:28-29, stating, "Him we proclaim, warning everyone and teaching everyone with all wisdom, that we may present everyone matures in Christ. For this, I toil, struggling with all his energy, which he powerfully works within me." Preaching that encourages spiritual growth helps believers become firmly rooted in Christ, bearing fruit and reflecting His character.

Preaching as discipleship also involves the development of spiritual disciplines and practices. Through preaching, believers are encouraged to engage in prayer, Bible study, worship, and other disciplines that deepen their relationship with God. The preacher's role is to impart knowledge and inspire and challenging believers to actively pursue a vibrant and transformative relationship with Christ.

Preaching as discipleship is vital to the church's mission to make disciples. It involves intentionally teaching and exposing God's Word to nurture believers, equip them for ministry, and foster spiritual growth and maturity. Through preaching, believers are instructed in biblical truths, guided in their application, and encouraged to live out their faith practically. Preaching as discipleship aligns with the Great Commission and the apostle Paul's emphasis on equipping and building up the body of Christ. By recognising the role of preaching in discipleship, the church can create an environment where believers continually grow in their faith, deepen their relationship with Christ, and actively participate in the work of the Kingdom.

Preaching as Evangelism

Preaching has a significant role in evangelism, which is the proclamation of the gospel message to those who have not yet embraced faith in Jesus Christ. Preaching as evangelism involves communicating the good news of salvation, inviting non-believers to respond in faith, and facilitating their entry into the Kingdom of God.

The foundation for preaching as evangelism can be found in Jesus' ministry. Throughout the Gospels, we see Jesus engaging in public preaching, proclaiming the arrival of the Kingdom of God and calling people to repentance and faith. In Mark 1:14-15, Jesus declares, "The time is fulfilled, and the kingdom of God is at hand; repent and believe in the gospel." Jesus' preaching had a clear evangelistic purpose, urging people to turn away from their sins and trust Him for salvation.

The early church also demonstrated the role of preaching in evangelism. In Acts 2, on Pentecost, Peter preached a powerful sermon that converted thousands of people. He boldly proclaimed the death and resurrection of Jesus, calling the listeners to repentance. Throughout the book of Acts, we see the apostles and early believers actively preaching to reach out to non-believers, share the message of salvation, and establish new churches.

Preaching as evangelism involves clearly communicating the gospel of Grace's message. The preacher proclaims the good news of Jesus Christ, highlighting His sacrificial death for the forgiveness of sins and His resurrection as the source of eternal life. The preacher explains the need for repentance, the call to faith in Christ, and the promise of salvation through Him. The power of the Holy Spirit works through the preached Word to convict hearts, draw people to God, and bring about genuine conversion.

Preaching as evangelism recognises the importance of addressing the questions, doubts, and objections that non-believers may have. The preacher seeks to engage with the intellectual, emotional, and spiritual barriers that hinder individuals from embracing the gospel. This may involve apologetic reasoning, addressing misconceptions about Christianity, and demonstrating the relevance and life-transforming power of the gospel message.

Preaching as evangelism is also characterised by urgency and compassion for the lost. The preacher recognises the eternal significance of salvation and the consequences of rejecting the gospel. The apostle Paul exemplified this urgency in his ministry, stating in 2 Corinthians 5:20, "Therefore, we are ambassadors for Christ, God making his appeal through us. On behalf of Christ, we implore you to be reconciled to God." Preachers are called to be ambassadors of Christ, pleading with non-believers to receive the message of reconciliation and turn to God in faith.

Preaching as evangelism is essential to the church's mission to reach the lost with the message of salvation. It follows the example of Jesus and the early church in boldly proclaiming the gospel, calling for repentance and faith. Preaching as evangelism involves clear communication of the gospel message, addressing the barriers that hinder non-believers, and demonstrating urgency and compassion for their salvation. By recognising the role of preaching in evangelism, the church can effectively bring people into a saving relationship with Jesus Christ.

9. Challenges and Opportunities in Preaching Today

In a rapidly changing world, preaching faces various challenges and opportunities. This chapter of our discussion focuses on exploring these dynamics and understanding how they impact the practice of preaching in today's context. As preachers navigate the complexities of the modern age, they encounter challenges to biblical authority, cultural changes and trends, and opportunities for Gospel impact. Preachers must grapple with these realities to effectively engage their congregations and communicate the timeless truths of God's Word.

This section will delve into the multifaceted challenges preachers face in upholding the authority of Scripture. We will examine how cultural shifts and trends can shape how people receive and perceive the message of the Gospel. We will explore the opportunities from embracing new platforms and methods to reach diverse audiences with the transformative power of God's Word. By recognising these challenges and seizing the opportunities, preachers can navigate the ever-changing landscape and faithfully fulfil their calling to proclaim the Good News.

Throughout history, preachers have encountered challenges to biblical authority, which remains relevant today. In an increasingly secular and sceptical society, the authority of Scripture may be questioned or undermined. Preachers must address doubts and misconceptions about the Bible, providing compelling reasons for its reliability and trustworthiness. The apostle Paul encourages Timothy, his protégé in ministry, to "preach the word; be ready in season and out of season; reprove, rebuke, and exhort, with complete patience and teaching" (2 Timothy 4:2). This admonition reminds preachers of the timeless importance of grounding their messages in the authority and truth of Scripture, even when faced with opposition or scepticism.

Cultural changes and trends also present challenges and opportunities for preachers. Society constantly evolves, and cultural values, beliefs, and norms are subject to transformation. Preachers must navigate these shifts with discernment, ensuring that the message of the Gospel remains relevant and impactful. The apostle Paul provides an example of contextualisation in his ministry. In 1 Corinthians 9:22, he writes, "I have become all things to all people, that by all means, I might save some." This verse emphasises the importance of understanding the cultural context and effectively communicating the Gospel within that framework while maintaining the integrity of the message.

Amidst these challenges, preachers have an array of opportunities for Gospel impact. Technological advancements and the rise of digital platforms provide new avenues for reaching wider audiences. Social media, podcasts, online streaming, and other digital tools allow preachers to engage with people beyond the confines of physical gatherings. Jesus Himself recognised the potential of leveraging technology when He said, "Go into all the world and proclaim the gospel to the whole creation" (Mark 16:15). Today, preachers can harness these tools to share the message of Christ with individuals who may have limited access to traditional church settings.

Cultural diversity and globalisation allow preachers to engage with various ethnicities, languages, and cultural backgrounds. The Gospel transcends boundaries and is for all people. The apostle Peter acknowledges this truth when he declares, "Truly I understand that God shows no partiality, but in every nation, anyone who fears him and does what is right is acceptable to him" (Acts 10:34-35). Preachers can embrace this diversity and tailor their messages to connect with different cultural contexts, effectively conveying the Gospel's transformative power across cultural barriers.

Our discussion in this chapter will focus on the challenges and opportunities preachers encounter in today's world. Preachers must address challenges to biblical authority, navigate cultural changes and trends, and leverage new platforms to effectively communicate the Gospel message.

Challenges to Biblical Authority

One of the significant challenges that preachers face in today's context is the questioning and undermining of biblical authority. In an increasingly secular and sceptical society, the reliability, relevance, and truth of Scripture may be called into question. This challenge requires preachers to address doubts, misconceptions, and objections and provide compelling reasons for the authority of God's Word.

The Bible itself affirms its authority and reliability. In 2 Timothy 3:16-17, the apostle Paul writes, "All Scripture is breathed out by God and profitable for teaching, reproof, correction, and training in righteousness, that the man of God may be complete, equipped for every good work." This verse emphasises that the Scriptures are not merely human writings but God-inspired. They hold the power to guide, instruct, and transform lives. As preachers, it is essential to affirm and proclaim the divine origin and authority of Scripture.

Addressing challenges to biblical authority requires engaging with various objections that may arise. For example, some may question certain passages' historical accuracy or scientific validity. Others may raise concerns about cultural and ethical differences between the Bible and modern society. Preachers must be equipped to provide reasoned responses, addressing these concerns while upholding the integrity and authority of God's Word.

One approach to addressing these challenges is through apologetics, which involves presenting a rational defence of the Christian faith. This includes offering historical evidence, archaeological discoveries, and logical reasoning that supports the credibility of the Bible. The apostle

Peter encourages believers to "always be prepared to make a defence to anyone who asks you for a reason for the hope that is in you" (1 Peter 3:15). By engaging in apologetics, preachers can equip themselves to address objections and reinforce the authority of Scripture.

Preachers can emphasise the internal consistency and coherence of the biblical message. Despite being written by multiple authors over thousands of years, the Bible presents a unified narrative pointing to God's redemptive work through Jesus Christ. Preachers can highlight the interconnectedness of Scripture, demonstrating how various passages and themes weave together to form a cohesive and compelling testimony.

In addressing challenges to biblical authority, preachers should also rely on the power of the Holy Spirit. The Spirit works in the hearts and minds of individuals, convicting them of the truth and opening their understanding of the message of Scripture. Jesus promised His disciples that the Holy Spirit would be their helper and guide in proclaiming the truth (John 14:26). Preachers must depend on the Holy Spirit's illumination to effectively communicate the authority and relevance of God's Word.

Ultimately, the challenges to biblical authority allow preachers to strengthen their understanding of Scripture and equip others to do the same. By addressing objections, providing reasoned responses, and relying on the Holy Spirit, preachers can effectively confront the challenges and uphold the enduring authority of God's Word in a sceptical world.

This chapter highlights the challenges that preachers face regarding biblical authority. Preachers need to address doubts, misconceptions, and objections by providing compelling reasons for the authority of Scripture. By engaging in apologetics, emphasising the coherence of Scripture, and relying on the Holy Spirit's guidance, preachers can effectively navigate these challenges and proclaim God's Word's enduring truth and authority.

Cultural Changes and Trends

Cultural changes and trends profoundly impact the practice of preaching in today's world. As societies evolve and adopt new values, beliefs, and norms, preachers must grapple with the challenge of effectively communicating the timeless truths of the Gospel in a culturally relevant manner. This section explores the dynamics of cultural changes and trends and how they intersect with the preaching ministry.

The Bible acknowledges the importance of cultural context in communication. The apostle Paul, in his letter to the Corinthian church, writes, "To the Jews, I became as a Jew, to win Jews. To those under the law, I became as one under the law... that I might win those under the law. To those outside the law, I became as one outside the law... that I might win those outside the law. To the weak I became weak, that I might win the weak" (1 Corinthians 9:20-22). Paul's approach demonstrates the need to understand and engage with the audience's cultural context to effectively communicate the Gospel.

In the face of cultural changes and trends, preachers must strive for contextualisation, which involves presenting the unchanging truths of Scripture in a way that resonates with the cultural framework of the hearers. This does not mean compromising the core message of the Gospel but rather adapting the methods, illustrations, and language to connect with the prevailing cultural context. By doing so, preachers can effectively bridge the gap between their audience's biblical worldview and cultural mindset.

However, contextualisation should always be balanced with the commitment to biblical integrity. While adapting to cultural changes, preachers must ensure that they do not dilute or compromise the essential truths of Scripture. The apostle Paul emphasises the importance of maintaining the purity of the Gospel when he writes, "But even if we or an angel from heaven should preach to you a gospel contrary to the one we preached to you, let him be accursed" (Galatians 1:8). This verse underscores the non-negotiable nature of the Gospel message, even during cultural shifts.

One aspect of cultural change that preachers must grapple with is the increasing relativism and subjectivity of truth. In a postmodern culture, absolute truth is often challenged, and individual experiences and perspectives take precedence. Preachers must navigate this challenge by presenting the timeless truths of Scripture as relevant and applicable to people's lives. The writer of Hebrews affirms the unchanging nature of God's Word, stating, "For the word of God is living and active, sharper than any two-edged sword" (Hebrews 4:12). This passage highlights the enduring power of God's Word, which can transcend cultural shifts and speak to the deepest needs of humanity.

Preachers must also be aware of the impact of technology and digital media on preaching. With the rise of social media, podcasts, online streaming, and other digital platforms, people's engagement with information and messages has changed significantly. Preachers can leverage these platforms to reach a wider audience and engage with individuals who may not have access to traditional church settings. Jesus' command to "go into all the world and proclaim the gospel to the whole creation" (Mark 16:15) takes on new dimensions in the digital age.

This section highlights the challenges, opportunities, cultural changes, and trends in the preaching ministry. Preachers must navigate the shifting cultural landscape by contextualising and adapting their approach to resonate with the cultural context while maintaining biblical integrity. They must address the relativism of truth by presenting the timeless truths of Scripture as relevant and applicable to people's lives. Preachers can leverage technology and digital platforms to reach a broader audience and extend the reach of the Gospel. By embracing these challenges and opportunities, preachers can effectively communicate the unchanging message of God's Word in a culturally relevant manner, impacting lives and transforming hearts.

Opportunities for Gospel Impact

While there are undoubtedly challenges in preaching, there are also significant opportunities for Gospel impact in today's world. Point 9.3 explores the various opportunities preachers can seize to proclaim the message of Jesus Christ and advance His Kingdom.

One of the key opportunities for Gospel impact lies in the growing hunger for spiritual fulfilment and meaning in people's lives. Despite the cultural shifts and secularisation, many individuals still seek answers to life's fundamental questions, long for a sense of purpose, and desire a deeper connection with the transcendent. As preachers, we have the privilege to offer the transformative message of the Gospel that addresses these longings. Jesus Himself declared, "I am the bread of life; whoever comes to me shall not hunger, and whoever believes in me shall never thirst" (John 6:35). By presenting Jesus as the ultimate source of fulfilment and meaning, preachers can engage with the deep spiritual needs of individuals and lead them to a life-giving relationship with Christ.

The diversity of today's globalised world presents a unique opportunity for cross-cultural and cross-ethnic preaching. As societies become more multicultural and interconnected, preachers have the chance to engage with individuals from various backgrounds and cultures. This aligns with the biblical vision of the Gospel transcending cultural and ethnic boundaries. The apostle Paul declares, "There is neither Jew nor Greek, there is neither slave nor free, there is no male and female, for you are all one in Christ Jesus" (Galatians 3:28). Preachers can celebrate and value the rich diversity of God's creation and extend the message of salvation to all people, regardless of their cultural or ethnic background.

Another opportunity for Gospel impact lies in social justice and compassion. Today's world is marked by various social, economic, and systemic issues, such as poverty, injustice, inequality, and discrimination. Preachers can actively engage with these issues and advocate for biblical principles of justice, mercy, and love. The prophet Micah succinctly captures God's desire for justice when he states, "He has told you, O man, what is good; and what does the LORD require of you but to do justice, and to love kindness, and to walk humbly with your God?" (Micah 6:8). By addressing these societal challenges from a biblical perspective, preachers can demonstrate the transformative power of the Gospel in both individual lives and the broader community.

The advancement of technology and digital platforms presents unique opportunities for reaching a wider audience and spreading the Gospel message. Through podcasts, online sermons, social media platforms, and live streaming, preachers can extend their reach beyond the confines of physical church buildings. Jesus commissioned His disciples to be witnesses "in Jerusalem and in all Judea and Samaria, and to the end of the earth" (Acts 1:8). The digital age provides a remarkable avenue for fulfilling this mission.

There are opportunities for collaboration and partnership in the preaching ministry. Preachers can join hands with other churches, ministries, and organisations to amplify their impact and reach. The apostle Paul speaks of the importance of unity and collaboration in the body of Christ, stating, "For just as the body is one and has many members, and all the members of the body, though many, are one body, so it is with Christ" (1 Corinthians 12:12). By working together, preachers can pool their resources, share insights and experiences, and make a more significant Kingdom impact.

This section highlights the abundant opportunities for Gospel impact in today's world. Preachers can engage with the hunger for spiritual fulfilment, embrace cross-cultural preaching, express compassion, leverage technology and digital platforms, and foster collaboration and partnership. By seizing these opportunities, preachers can effectively proclaim the transformative message of the Gospel, impact lives, and advance the Kingdom of God. It is a time of great potential and possibility for the preaching ministry as we strive to be faithful ambassadors of Christ in a world that needs His saving grace and love.

10. Conclusion and Final Thoughts

The journey of exploring the art and practice of preaching comes to a close with this chapter, which concludes our comprehensive study. This section offers a space for reflection, encouragement, and a vision for the future of preaching. It is an opportunity to summarise the key learnings and insights gained throughout the book and leave preachers with a renewed sense of purpose and inspiration.

Preaching is not merely a skill or technique but a sacred calling and a vital ministry within the Church. It is a divine task entrusted to imperfect vessels who seek to faithfully proclaim God's Word and lead His people in their spiritual journey. As we conclude this book, we are reminded of the words of the apostle Paul to his protégé Timothy: "Preach the word; be ready in season and out of season; reprove, rebuke, and exhort, with complete patience and teaching" (2 Timothy 4:2). These words encapsulate the timeless charge for preachers to faithfully and boldly proclaim the truth of Scripture, irrespective of the cultural and temporal context.

In this final section, we will take the opportunity to reflect on the transformative power of preaching and its integral role in the life of the Church. We will encourage preachers to continue growing in their personal and spiritual lives, reminding them of the necessity of ongoing prayer, dependence on the Holy Spirit, and a commitment to personal character development. We will emphasise the importance of self-evaluation and seeking feedback from others to continuously grow and improve the preaching ministry.

We will explore the future of preaching, recognising the evolving landscape of our world and the emerging challenges and opportunities that lie ahead. As culture and society change, preachers must remain anchored in the unchanging truth of God's Word while being adaptable and relevant in their communication. We will explore the potential impact of technology, changing demographics, and cultural shifts on the practice of preaching. This will include considerations for preaching in an increasingly digital world and reaching diverse audiences with cultural sensitivity and biblical fidelity.

Ultimately, the conclusion of this book aims to inspire preachers to persevere in their calling, equipping them with renewed vision and passion. We will remind them of the significance of their role in leading the Church in worship, discipleship, and evangelism. Preaching is not a solitary endeavour but a communal effort that calls for collaboration, support, and encouragement among preachers and congregations.

As we embark on this final section, let us be reminded of the words of the psalmist who declared, "I will sing of steadfast love and justice; to you, O LORD, I will make music" (Psalm 101:1). May our preaching be characterised by a deep love for God and His people, an unwavering commitment to truth and justice, and a desire to bring glory to the name of our Lord Jesus Christ. Let us journey together in reflection, encouragement, and anticipation for the future of preaching, confident that our labour in the Word is never in vain.

Encouragement to Preachers

In the book's final section, we focus on encouraging preachers. Preaching is a noble calling, but it can also be a demanding and challenging task. It requires dedication, perseverance, and a deep reliance on God's strength. In this section, we aim to uplift and inspire preachers, reminding them of the significance of their ministry and offering practical encouragement to sustain them in their journey.

First and foremost, preachers are reminded of the foundational truth that their calling is not their own but a divine appointment from God. Jeremiah received a specific calling from God to be a prophet to the nations, and he initially felt inadequate for the task. However, God reassured him, saying, "Before I formed you in the womb, I knew you; before you were born, I set you apart; I appointed you as a prophet to the nations" (Jeremiah 1:5). This biblical example reminds preachers that their calling is not based on their own abilities or qualifications but on God's sovereign choice. It reminds us that God equips those He calls and that preachers can find confidence and strength in His guidance.

Preachers are encouraged to cultivate a deep and vibrant relationship with God. The effectiveness of preaching is not merely in the eloquence of words but in the power of the Holy Spirit working through the preacher. Jesus said to His disciples, "But you will receive power when the Holy Spirit comes upon you, and you will be my witnesses in Jerusalem and in all Judea and Samaria, and to the end of the earth" (Acts 1:8). Preachers are called to rely on the Holy Spirit for guidance, wisdom, and anointing in their preaching ministry. Cultivating a life of prayer, seeking the presence of God, and being sensitive to the leading of the Holy Spirit is essential for preachers to be effective in their proclamation of the Gospel.

Preachers are reminded of the need for personal growth and continual development. The apostle Paul exhorted his young disciple, Timothy, saying, "Do your best to present yourself to God as one approved, a worker who has no need to be ashamed, rightly handling the word of truth" (2 Timothy 2:15). Preachers are called to be diligent students of the Word, continually growing in their understanding of Scripture, theology, and the cultural context in which they minister. This involves engaging in regular study, reading, and attending conferences or courses to sharpen their preaching skills and deepen their knowledge of God's Word.

In addition to personal growth, preachers are encouraged to seek support and accountability from fellow believers. Proverbs remind us that "iron sharpens iron, and one man sharpens another" (Proverbs 27:17). Preachers can benefit greatly from other trusted individuals' insights, feedback, and encouragement. This can come through mentorship relationships, participation in preaching forums or groups, or even seeking feedback from congregants. Constructive criticism and support from fellow believers can help preachers refine their preaching style, address blind spots, and improve their effectiveness.

Lastly, preachers are reminded to find rest and renewal in God. Ministry can be demanding, and preachers may face burnout or discouragement. Jesus Himself modelled the importance of rest and solitude in His ministry. He said, "Come to me, all who labour and are heavily laden, and I will give you rest" (Matthew 11:28). Preachers are encouraged to prioritise self-care, maintain healthy boundaries, and seek spiritual refreshing and renewal times. This can include regular rest periods, engaging in activities that bring joy and relaxation, participating in spiritual retreats or seeking guidance from spiritual mentors.

This section highlights the importance of encouragement for preachers. It reminds them of the divine calling on their lives, the necessity of relying on the Holy Spirit, the significance of personal growth, the value of accountability and support from fellow believers, and the need for rest and renewal. By embracing these aspects, preachers can find renewed strength, inspiration, and endurance in their ministry. Ultimately, the goal is to uplift preachers, reminding them of their vital role in proclaiming the Gospel and encouraging them to press on with perseverance and joy. As the apostle Paul writes in Galatians 6:9, "And let us not grow weary of doing good, for in due season we will reap if we do not give up." May preachers be encouraged to continue sowing the seeds of God's Word, knowing their labour will bear fruit soon.

Vision for the Future of Preaching

In the book's final section, we focus on the future of preaching. The landscape of our world is continually changing, and the challenges and opportunities facing preachers are also evolving. This section explores a vision for the future of preaching, calling preachers to adapt, innovate, and remain faithful to their calling amid cultural shifts.

One of the fundamental principles to consider when envisioning the future of preaching is the unchanging nature of God's Word. The author of Hebrews reminds us, "For the word of God is living and active, sharper than any two-edged sword, piercing to the division of soul and of spirit, of joints and of marrow, and discerning the thoughts and intentions of the heart" (Hebrews 4:12). Despite societal changes, the Word of God remains a powerful force that brings transformation and conviction. Preachers are called to uphold the authority and relevance of Scripture, unswayed by cultural pressures or shifting trends. The future of preaching should be rooted in a commitment to faithfully proclaim the unchanging truth of God's Word, addressing the spiritual needs of people in every generation.

In the context of technological advancements, preachers are encouraged to harness the power of digital tools and platforms for the sake of the Gospel. The digital age has brought about new opportunities for communication and outreach. Preachers can use social media, podcasts, online streaming, and other digital mediums to reach a broader audience and engage with people beyond the church's walls. The apostle Paul's approach to adapting to the cultural context is exemplified in his statement, "I have become all things to all people, that by all means, I might save some" (1 Corinthians 9:22). Preachers can embrace technology as a means to effectively communicate the message of Christ, making use of modern tools without compromising the message or diluting its impact.

The future of preaching requires a heightened cultural sensitivity and understanding. As societies become more diverse and multicultural, preachers are called to navigate the complexities of different cultural contexts. The apostle Peter reminds us, "But in your hearts honour Christ the Lord as holy, always being prepared to make a defence to anyone who asks you for a reason for the hope that is in you; yet do it with gentleness and respect" (1 Peter 3:15). Preachers must be attuned to the specific needs, questions, and concerns of the people they are ministering to. They should strive to communicate the Gospel's timeless truths in relatable and meaningful ways within various cultural settings.

In addition to cultural sensitivity, the future of preaching necessitates a commitment to holistic ministry. Preaching should not be seen as a standalone event but as part of a broader discipleship process. Preachers are called to equip and empower believers to live out their faith in all aspects of life. The apostle Paul writes to the Ephesians, "Rather, speaking the truth in love, we are to grow up in every way into him who is the head, into Christ" (Ephesians 4:15). Preachers should not only focus on delivering inspiring sermons but also on nurturing spiritual growth, providing pastoral care, and fostering community within the church. The future of preaching holds immense potential for spreading the transformative power of the Gospel, connecting with diverse audiences, and igniting a revival of faith that transcends cultural barriers and reaches the hearts of people around the world.

The future of preaching is marked by the unwavering commitment to the authority and relevance of God's Word, adapting to the changing cultural landscape, leveraging digital tools and platforms, embracing cultural sensitivity, and engaging in holistic ministry. As preachers look to the future, they are called to remain faithful to the timeless truths of Scripture while creatively and effectively communicating the message of Christ in a rapidly evolving world. The vision for the future of preaching is rooted in the Great Commission given by Jesus Himself: "Go therefore and make disciples of all nations, baptising them in the name of the Father and of the Son and of the Holy Spirit, teaching them to observe all that I have commanded you" (Matthew 28:19-20). Preachers are entrusted with the sacred task of proclaiming the Gospel and equipping believers for discipleship. By embracing this vision, preachers can continue to impact lives, transform communities, and advance the Kingdom of God in future generations.

Preaching, Pastoral Care and Technology

The tension between embracing technology and providing pastoral care arises from the potential for technology to create a sense of distance or impersonality in pastoral relationships. While technology offers incredible opportunities for communication, connection, and ministry outreach, it can also present challenges regarding pastoral care's personal and intimate aspects.

One of the primary concerns is the risk of depersonalisation that technology can bring. When pastoral care is solely mediated through digital platforms, there is a possibility of losing genuine human connection and the depth of relationship from face-to-face interaction. The apostle Paul highlights the importance of personal presence and relational connection in pastoral ministry when he writes to the Thessalonians, "So, being affectionately desirous of you, we were ready to share with you not only the gospel of God but also our own selves, because you had become very dear to us" (1 Thessalonians 2:8). Pastoral care involves the ministry of presence, empathy, and personal investment in the lives of individuals. Technology should enhance, not replace, these essential aspects of pastoral care.

The limitations of technology can hinder the full scope of pastoral care. Digital communication, while efficient and convenient, may not always allow for the same depth of understanding, discernment, and support that can be achieved through in-person interactions. Non-verbal cues, physical presence, and a sense of shared space contribute to a more comprehensive pastoral care experience. The apostle John recognises the significance of personal interaction when he writes, "Though I have much to write to you, I would rather not use paper and ink. Instead, I hope to come to you and talk face to face, so that our joy may be complete" (2 John 1:12). Face-to-face encounters provide opportunities for deeper connection, active listening, and the ability to respond holistically to the spiritual, emotional, and physical needs of individuals.

However, it is essential to recognise that technology can support and enhance pastoral care. It can provide avenues for ongoing communication, spiritual resources, and virtual community building. It can facilitate access to counselling, prayer support, and biblical teaching across geographical distances. The key is to balance utilising technology as a tool while maintaining the relational and personal aspects of pastoral care.

In navigating this tension, pastors and church leaders should approach technology with discernment and wisdom, mindful of its potential benefits and limitations. They should prioritise in-person interactions whenever possible, recognising the unique value of personal presence and attentive listening. At the same time, they can leverage technology to supplement pastoral care efforts, extend the reach of ministry, and provide resources for spiritual growth. Ultimately, the goal is integrating technology to support and enhance pastoral care while preserving the relational dynamics central to effective ministry and discipleship.

Bibliography

———

1. Craddock, Fred B. Preaching. Nashville: Abingdon Press, 1985.
2. Greidanus, Sidney. Preaching Christ from the Old Testament: A Contemporary Hermeneutical Method. Grand Rapids: Eerdmans, 1999.
3. Robinson, Haddon W. Biblical Preaching: The Development and Delivery of Expository Messages. Grand Rapids: Baker Academic, 2014.
4. Stott, John R. W. Between Two Worlds: The Challenge of Preaching Today. Grand Rapids: Eerdmans, 1982.
5. Chapell, Bryan. Christ-Centered Preaching: Redeeming the Expository Sermon. Grand Rapids: Baker Academic, 2005.
6. Long, Thomas G. The Witness of Preaching. Louisville: Westminster John Knox Press, 2005.
7. Keller, Timothy. Preaching: Communicating Faith in an Age of Skepticism. New York: Viking, 2015.
8. Adams, Jay E. Preaching with Purpose: The Urgent Task of Homiletics. Phillipsburg: P&R Publishing, 1986.
9. Carson, D. A. Exegetical Fallacies. Grand Rapids: Baker Academic, 1996.
10. Hughes, R. Kent. Preaching the Word: Hebrews—An Anchor for the Soul. Wheaton: Crossway, 2017.
11. Koller, Charles W. How to Preach without Notes. Grand Rapids: Baker Books, 2007.
12. Larson, Craig Brian, and Haddon Robinson. The Art and Craft of Biblical Preaching. Grand Rapids: Zondervan, 2005.
13. Lowry, Eugene L. The Homiletical Plot: The Sermon as Narrative Art Form. Louisville: Westminster John Knox Press,

2001.

14. Wilson, Paul Scott. The Four Pages of the Sermon: A Guide to Biblical Preaching. Nashville: Thomas Nelson, 1999.

15. Willimon, William H. Preaching and Leading Worship: Pastors and Laypeople on Liturgical Practice. Nashville: Abingdon Press, 2009.

About the Author

Dr Andrew J. Lamont-Turner: Theological Scholar, Pastor, Author, and Teacher

Andrew Lamont-Turner is a theological scholar, author, and Bible teacher who has dedicated his life to pursuing theological knowledge and disseminating spiritual wisdom. With a profound understanding of the scriptures and a passion for teaching, Andrew has emerged as a supportive voice in the field of theology. His extensive academic qualifications and love for God and his family have shaped him into a multifaceted individual committed to nurturing spiritual growth and intellectual exploration.

Academic Journey: Andrew's academic journey reflects his thirst for theological understanding. He holds a Bachelor of Theology, Bachelor of Theology (Honours), Master of Theology, and a Doctor of Philosophy in Theology. These qualifications represent years of rigorous study and a commitment to excellence in his field. Andrew's intellectual curiosity extends beyond theology, as he also possesses a Bachelor of Education (Honours) and several Postgraduate Certificates in various commercial fields. This interdisciplinary approach has enriched his perspective and broadened his ability to connect theological principles with everyday life.

Teaching and Writing: Andrew's knowledge of theology has been expressed through his teaching and writing endeavours. As an educator, he has inspired countless students through his engaging lectures and insights into the scriptures. His ability to distil complex theological concepts into accessible teachings has garnered him a reputation as an exceptional communicator.

In addition to his teaching, Andrew is a prolific author who has published several books and a comprehensive Bible study series. His books explore various aspects of Christian theology, offering insights, practical guidance, and thought-provoking reflections. With meticulous research, clear exposition, and a genuine desire to bridge the gap between academic theology and everyday faith, Andrew's writings have touched the lives of many, nurturing their spiritual growth and deepening their understanding of God's Word.

Pastoral Leadership: Living his faith ensures Andrew takes his Pastoral Leadership very seriously. He is the Pastor of a community church in rural South Africa, where he ensures the flock entrusted to him by God is well-fed and looked after.

Family and Faith: Beyond his academic pursuits, Andrew cherishes his loving husband and father role. His unwavering commitment to his family has been a source of strength and inspiration throughout his journey. Andrew's faith in God is the bedrock of his life, infusing every aspect of his work and relationships. His deep conviction in the transformative power of the Gospel of Grace resonates in his writing and teaching, making him a relatable teacher for those seeking to deepen their spiritual walk.